Technology Resources For Growing Businesses 2011

RAMON RAY
Editor & Technology Evangelist,
Smallbiztechnology.com

smallbiz
technology
tech insight & news for small business

Contents

Introduction   09

Chapter 1:
**Three Rules For Using Technology
Strategically In Your Business**   11
Technology is an Investment. Not a Cost.   12
Outsource Your Technology Expertise   13
Don't Technologize a Bad Business Process   14

Chapter 2:
Social Media 101   15
Benefits of Social Media   16
Facebook   17
LinkedIn   18
Twitter   19
How Do I Start with Social Media?   20
Build Listening Stations   20
Etiquette   22
Why "Follower Count" is Not Important   22
Social Media Resources   24

Chapter 3:
Mobility and Your Business   25
Don't Buy Based on the Cool Factor   26
What Do You Do and Who are You?   26
Five Corners of Mobility   26
Mobile Operating Systems   27
Hardware   29
Mobile Security   32
Wireless Carrier   33
Connectivity   33
Applications   34
Mobile Computing Resources   35

Chapter 4:
Customer Relationship Management (CRM)   37
Automation   37
CRM Is Simple: Know Your Customers   38
Traditional CRM vs. Social CRM   39
CRM Resources   43

Chapter 5:
Protecting Your Data   45
What Needs to be Secured?   46
Data Security Tools   47
Backup and Recovery 101   51
Protecting Your Data Resources   54

Chapter 6:
Building Business Class Web Sites   55
Focus on the Customer   56
Have a Plan   57
Choosing a Name   57
Make Navigation Easy   58
Make It Informative   59
Security   60
Easy Customer Contact   60
Keep it Fresh   61
Be Found   62
Be Simple: KIS (Keep It Simple)   62
Building Business Class Web Sites Resources   63

Chapter 7:
Online Marketing & Advertising   65
Types of Advertising   66
Online Advertising Components   67
Search Engine Optimization   68
Advertising Channels   69
Online Marketing and Advertising Resources   74

Chapter 8:
Email Marketing   75
Dating Your Leads and Marrying Your Customers   75
Email Newsletter Marketing Tips   76
Why Use An Email Marketing Service   78
Beyond Email Marketing As Usual   78
Email Marketing Resources   80

Chapter 9:
Blogging for Business   81
Fresh Content   82
Community and Communication   83
Blogging Resources   83

Chapter 10:
Video For Business 85
Expertise 86
Video Equipment 86
Hosting 87
Two Neat Video Services 87
Video Resources 87

Chapter 11:
Software As A Service (SaaS) 89
How Cloud Computing Helped Boost Productivity
In the Mountains of Pennsylvania 90
9 Questions To Ask Before Moving To Cloud
Computing 91
What Services Are Ideal For Cloud Computing 92
Software As A Service (SaaS) Resources 95

Chapter 12:
Printers 97
Speed 98
Paper Handling 98
Ink and Toner 98
Color or Black and White 98
Ink Jet or Laser Jet 99
Multi-function Printers 99
Printer Buying Resources 99

Chapter 13:
**Money Saving Tips for Your Business
When Investing In Technology** 101
Purchase and Support 102
Power, Cooling, and Space 102
IT System/Network Administration/Management 102
Hardware 103
Software 104
Networking and Communications 104
Telephony 104
Storage 105
Printers 105

Summary 107

Acknowledgments 108

Photo Courtesy of NYIT Magazine

I am blessed to have been using technology for many years. Since the late 1980s I've been using a variety of online services (Prodigy, AOL, Earthlink, TIAC) and fiddling around with all sorts of computers and accessories.

The evolution of technology has been amazing. From my Casio Data Bank Watch (similar to this one here: http://www.casio.com/products/Timepiece/Databank/DBC310-1/) and the Sharp WIZARD of 1988 (http://en.wikipedia.org/wiki/Sharp_Wizard) to the Palm Handspring Visor (in 1999) and beyond, I've enjoyed how technology has always made business professionals and consumers more productive.

There are many of you who find technology to be downright frustrating and confusing. You know you need technology but you still find it a "black hole" and something that only your nieces or geeks can delve into.

Hopefully this guide will whet your appetite for leveraging technology in your business, help you learn how to use it and seek the help of experts when you need it.

RAMON RAY

CHAPTER 1:
Three Rules for Using Technology Strategically in Your Business

When implementing technology in your business, keep in mind that technology is ONLY a tool. Technology in and of itself will not make your business more productive or boost sales. These three rules I've developed are just guidelines to help you in your journey of using technology.

1 Technology is an Investment, Not a Cost.

You spend money on insurance, right? You have a lawyer (most likely) and an accountant (for sure), right? However, when it comes to spending money on technology, sometimes we ONLY spend money if we have to. Instead of spending money on technology to fix an immediate need, you should INVEST in technology for today and the future.

Purchase technology as an investment in your future business growth. Sure, some technology you must have, like a computer monitor. But what about technology to help you better understand who your customers are and how to better sell them what they are most likely to buy—such as business analytics software?

If you are building a business that's **built to last,** you must think of your technology spending as an investment in how technology can help your business GROW. You must spend money on technology that will help you now and in the future (yep, I said it twice).

The right investments in technology will help you save money, save time, do more with less and, overall, grow your business.

Don't think of where your business is now, but think of where your business could be in two to three years and invest in technology accordingly.

In order to properly purchase technology as an investment, and not as a cost, you must invest in technology as you would in the stock market—mutual funds or otherwise.

You need to measure the results and know past performance which is a good indicator of future results. You also need to have a plan of action. Are you considering an aggressive growth strategy in your business or are you planning on staying small? Are you planning on serving many more customers, but hope to keep the same staffing levels?

When you buy technology make sure you know what you want to achieve with it and that you have some type of benchmark to know where you stand prior to the technology investment. For example, if you're buying a new phone system because 50 phone calls per day are being lost and not routed to your voice response system, you need to take note of this. After the telephone system is installed and sufficient time is given for the installation (including training) to be fully implemented, then measure the results. Are phone calls still being dropped? Have things improved? Are more phone calls being properly routed to your voice response system?

2 Outsource Your Technology Expertise

There is NO need for you to manage and implement technology on your own.

You are an expert in what you sell (whether you're a florist, computer vendor, lawyer, graphic artist, or media consultant). But you are not an expert in network security, data backup, or mobile technology.

The only way you are going to maximize your use of technology is to outsource your implementation of it. You should outsource technology, like other things in your business, for two main reasons:

1. **To save time** - For example: you don't want to take the time to learn how to build a web site and then take the time to build it. Your time is better spent on the core aspect of growing your business while you hire a web designer to build your web site.

2. **For expertise** - Using the web site building example, it'd be near impossible for your web design skills (assuming you are not a web developer) to compete with that of a professional web developer. It's best to hire an expert who can build you the best web site your budget can afford, with the functionality you need.

Technology is not all that you need to outsource.

If you find that you are scanning business cards, answering phones, and faxing proposals, you need to hire someone else to do these tasks for you so you can concentrate on your business. If you are a one-person business or a 50-person business, you need to manage your company and concentrate on its growth. Hire someone else, like a smart virtual or in-person assistant, or just another person, to help you mange tasks that are not central to what you need to do to grow your business.

Companies like Elance help you find and manage the talent you need to grow your business.

Outsourcing your technology expertise does not mean that you can't do things yourself. It means you are RELYING on a technology expert to guide you and ensure you are implementing the right technology for your business, at the right time.

" **...if there are parts of your business that are not going so well and you think technology is the answer, you're probably wrong."**

3

Don't Technologize a Bad Business Process

I'm sure you run a very good business and do your best to manage its various processes. However, if there are parts of your business that are not going so well and you think technology is the answer, you're probably wrong.

Most of the time, it's not technology first and foremost that a business needs to improve. It's a business process. For example: if sales are down, it's not that you necessarily need a CRM solution or a better designed web site. You might need a better sales process, a better sales team, or a better marketing plan instead. Once the CORE of the plan to boost your sales is in order, you can then consider what technology to implement. Having a CRM solution to help manage customer relations, or a better web site to help customers find what products they want to buy, and purchasing key words on a search engine can then be considered as they fit into your marketing plan.

This is only an example, but the same principle should be followed in using technology in every aspect of your business.

CHAPTER 2:
Social Media 101

There are a variety of definitions of what social media is and what it is not.

Social media, as far as YOUR business is concerned, is a host of online services and tools that help you to connect with people and enable a discussion with people of common interests. This could be local skate boarders tweeting about the best skate parks in the city or lawyers across the country tweeting about the latest Supreme Court ruling.

Benefits of Social Media
Social Media communication can be used to:

» Directly drive sales (listing daily coupons, alerting an audience to sales incentives, etc.)

» Remind people of the company's products and services (similar to what many email newsletters do)—or branding

» Provide technical support to customers (customers helping customers and the company helping customers)

» Obtain customer intelligence and insight on the company's products and services (what product customers like, or maybe finding out that customers are using a product in a different way than the company is selling it)

» Nurture a community of evangelists who are the most ardent fans of the company's brand/product/ services and help them use "digital word of mouth" to reach other customers (similar to how Barack Obama's campaign leveraged social media)

» Help drive traffic to your website with real time search playing a larger role in SERP (search engine results page), if getting your website to rank is important, social media activity will not only help you in the rankings, it will also help you drive traffic to your website.

» Turn cold calls into warm calls. These social media sites remove the barriers of entry that you experience in the physical world. There are no secretaries or receptionists to get past. You can reach out and communicate directly with the decision makers/buyers. With the information you can glean from their profiles and activity, you will be able to have a more meaningful conversation from the start.

These are just a few examples. But if you want to sell, find customers, obtain leads, or nurture existing customers, social media is a great way to do this.

The most widely used social media networks are:

FACEBOOK (www.facebook.com) - its core strength is keeping up to date with your network of friends and sharing photos, videos, updates, links, and all sorts of applications and games to enrich the experience. Business can have a similar experience with customers through Facebook pages.

LINKEDIN (www.linkedin.com)- is all about helping professionals find each other through their network of "connections" and discussing things, in groups, of interest to them.

TWITTER (www.twitter.com) - useful for people who want to keep up to date with a person or business. Communication is via short (140 characters or less) updates or "tweets" from that person (or business).

The best way to start using social media is to LISTEN. Unlike email or chat, social media is a technology which enables people to find other people of common interest and communicate with them, in real time (or near real time).

As you begin your journey of social media, if you dive right in and try to talk, you'll be as bad as the folks at a party or reception who barge into other people's conversations without the courtesy of first listening to what is being talked about and then engaging in thoughtful conversation.

Facebook

Facebook is a great tool for building a community around a certain topic, theme, or interest. This is why, increasingly, companies are giving Facebook web site addresses, such as www.facebook.com/honda, instead of www.honda.com.

Facebook enables you to see other friends of yours in this community (or group or page), post photos, videos, and more. It is an ideal community builder. The ability to post events and causes and so many more features makes it a hub of communication for professionals and not just friends and family. Businesses can also leverage Facebook to lead visitors to their web sites, whether they're shopping for a book or browsing for a plumber, and connect with their friends who have also visited the web site. Maybe if your friends like something, you'll like it too.

Facebook continues to add features that can help you promote your business. It has an advertising platform that provides highly targeted pay per click advertising as well. (See page 66). This helps to better ensure that your advertisement is directly targeted to those who meet a certain criteria based on location, age, likes, and others things.

LinkedIn

LinkedIn is all about connecting to other professionals and is still the preeminent source for finding a job, finding a person's contact information, and for employee recruitment. As a sales and marketing tool, the power of LinkedIn is that since so many professionals have profiles on LinkedIn, you can find just about anyone you need to be in touch with. Recently I've found that using LinkedIn's groups is great. LinkedIn has thousands of groups on a variety of topics and I've found that many of the discussions, especially within moderated groups, are robust, very professional, and informative. Check out the Questions & Answers section as this is a rich resource of people asking questions. You might just have the answer.

BIG LINKEDIN TIP: Have as full a LinkedIn profile as you can and have a good-looking picture. Not some cheap, crackerjack, cell phone, blurred photo.

Linkedin also has applications that empower members to share relevant and timely information, find and promote events, follow a company for up-to-date changes, and goes as far as to recommend people to connect with and groups to join.

Linkedin also has a powerful target advertising system that enables you to select by geography, title, company size, and more to help ensure that only your target audience sees your ad. This helps you maximize your PPC (pay per click) spend for optimal effect.

Twitter

Twitter, with its limit of 140 characters, is one of the best ways to LISTEN to conversations about your business or industry. It's also a great way to provide quick insight and tips or links to web sites to your followers. Use a tool like TweetDeck (http://www.tweetdeck.com), HootSuite (http://hoot-suite.com/), Postling (http://www.postling.com), or Dlvr.it (http://www.dlvr.it) to help you manage multiple searches, such as your name, business name, competitors, and industry keywords. These tools can also help you manage the stream of incoming tweets so you can stay on top of those that are important to your business and also allows you to manage your posts to Twitter (and other social networks).

HOT TIP

Twitter enables you to "dive into" the conversation on a particular topic and as relevant, point users to great resources on your own web site.

How Do I Start With Social Media?

Knowing where to invest your time is often the first challenge. Although a social media strategy should incorporate multiple sites since not everyone is on any single site, investing your time wisely will help you to reap dividends early on. One recommendation is to start with the world you know. You can upload your contacts into a service site like flowtown.com to see where your current contacts are engaging and start there. It will often depend on the demographics of your customers which sites they use most.

Having a content strategy is also another excellent way to prepare for a social media engagement. It is a good idea to share material and content other than your own marketing material. You can find industry sites, news, blogs, and websites online to help you with sharable content. Other valuable sites are blog and news aggregators such as alltop.com.

Build Listening Stations

Learning to listen is important not only to start, but also to sustain a meaningful, productive and effective marketing strategy. Set up google.com/alerts so that you are immediately made aware of any breaking news or information about you, your company, key accounts, and prospects. Another effective tool is to set

> **Having a content strategy is also another excellent way to prepare for a social media engagement. It is a good idea to share material and content other than your own marketing material."**

up "listening stations" for top prospects and accounts. This can also help you find people to follow and connect with, in addition to knowing what they are talking about.

Here are some steps to do that:

1. Set up a Gmail account or use any RSS 'reader' *
2. Set up Google Reader (google.com/reader)
3. Set up a separate folder in reader for a particular company/ person's name and or keywords
4. Search for names and keywords at Technorati.com (a blog search engine), and when the results come up, right click on the RSS button and select "copy link location"
5. Go back to Google Reader and click the blue plus button

and paste what you copied from Technorati (the search link) and paste into your reader

6. Go to blogsearch.google.com and repeat as above, copying and pasting links to different RSS feeds from your search results into the reader
7. search.twitter.com and repeat as above
8. Try Youtube, Flickr, Socialmention, etc. and repeat as above
9. Repeat for each person / company / keyword or phrase
10. Now you've added a bunch of information sources about your topic and can follow them all in one place through the RSS reader

Readers: Google, RSS Bandit, Mozilla Thunderbird, Attensa for Outlook, Firefox, Newsgator, Rojo, etc.

On Facebook, create a page for your business. Use this page to post information about your business, including interesting photos and video. Also post information about your customers, their own businesses, and how they are using your product in their business. Imagine a water cooler or community, but online.

Make sure you get the word out about your Facebook page to everyone—your customers, your vendors, and partners, and of course your employees. Encourage everyone to participate.

On Twitter, first create an account. Then use Twitter's search function (search.twitter.com) to start listing your name, your company name, competition, your industry, etc. After a few hours, or maybe a few days, you'll start to get a sense of the conversation happening online. Don't kick yourself for not do-ing this sooner. Start engaging in conversation with others. Talk about yourself/your business but ALSO give information about other things, even competitors. It's a CONVERSATION. Be a re-source. (And please include a nice photo.)

CHECK OUT: chris Brogan's insight on Twitter for Business here:
http://www.chrisbrogan.com/50_ideas_on_using_twitter_for_business/

Getting started on LinkedIn is equally simple. Create a pro-file, make sure you include your photo and make your profile as robust as possible. Find people to link to. There are options to upload your address book and let LinkedIn help you connect with others. But don't worry, after a few hours or days, people will find you and ask to connect to you. Search for discussion groups to participate in. Don't post about yourself and ask people to buy from you. Instead, treat it like a real conversation. Read the discussion threads. Join in by giving advice and insight. Be known online as a resource of information and referrals. Follow the discussion group rules.

CHECK OUT: workerdaily lists 33 ways to use LinkedIn for business here: http://gigaom.com/collaboration/33_ways_to_use_linkedin_for_business/

Etiquette
There is nothing more disheartening than investing time into a social media program and getting blocked or blacklisted. To avoid losing your audience, follow some basic best practices:
- » Be respectful and helpful - Never flame (post in anger, get negative, use unprofessional language, etc.)
- » Don't SPAM - Sell, sell, sell. No one likes to be sold to. A 20-to-1 ratio of helpful and other content in your marketing posts is important
- » Don't make it about minutiae (what you ate for breakfast, the TV show you are watching)
- » Comment (positively) on others posts; share their content with your audience.
- » Respect others – Don't complain about others; don't spread rumors or gossip

Why "Follower Count" is Not Important
You might be tempted to get caught up in how many followers you have, especially on Twitter. Don't. While follower count is important and can be a measure of popularity or interest, it's not everything.

Megan Berry, Marketing Manager for Klout shares these three important points:
1. **Most followers don't really follow you.** I hope I'm not bursting your bubble, but clicking that follow button doesn't mean someone cares about you or your business. It doesn't mean they're reading your tweets. It doesn't mean they'll ever click your links. Many people follow thousands, if not tens of thousands of people. It is impossible to read that many tweets. If they've never engaged with you, it's probably because they're not paying attention.

2. **It's too easy to game.** You can see the extreme example of this above, but anyone can fall victim to this trap. If all you care about are followers, you set up the wrong incentives for yourself (or your business). Want more followers quickly? Follow people, or have a Twitter contest, or create a method that makes people follow your account when they sign up for your service. You may want to do all of these things, but the reason shouldn't be solely about getting followers.

3. **So, how should you measure Twitter success?** That will vary based on your goals. Your metrics will vary if you're looking for brand awareness vs better customer service vs. leads. My suggestion is to focus on tangible actions instead of follows. How many people message you, retweet you, or click on your links? Of course, I have to suggest checking out Klout because we measure Twitter influence based on action (bias alert: I work there), but either way just, please, don't only look at follower count.

Read Megan's full article on Smallbiztechnology.com here: http://smallbiztechnology.com/archive/2010/07/why-follower-count-is-a-lousy.html

" Focus on tangible actions instead of follows. How many people message you, retweet you, or click on your links?"

Social Media Resources

Dell's Social Media Page
http://www.facebook.com/dellsocialmedia

Microsoft Office Live's Social Media eBook by John Jantsch
http://smallbusiness.officelive.com/social-media/ebook/

Inc Technology "Social Media for Business Sake" article
http://technology.inc.com/internet/articles/200804/leary.html

Batch Book's Social Media for Small Business
http://www.batchblue.com/bluepaper-socialmedia.html

Bumble Bee LLC
What is a social Media Strategy
http://bumblebeellc.com/serendipity/index.php?/archives/103-Just-What-is-a-Social-Media-Strategy.html

Generating Leads Through Linkedin
http://bumblebeellc.com/serendipity/index.php?/archives/96-Generating-Leads-Through-Linkedin.html

CHAPTER 3:
Mobility and Your Business

Being cocooned in your office all day might be delightful to many, but it's hardly practical for most business owners who want to grow their business. You have to get out, meet customers, visit suppliers, and go on extended business trips.

When you do, it's important that you can operate your business as well out of your office as you do in your office.

Mobility is so important because competitors are only a mouse click away. Budgets are severely restricted. Customers demand a fast response—this means in minutes or hours and NOT the next day or "when I get back to my office."

When going mobile, you need to consider the following key factors:

» Mobile hardware (such as computer, netbook and/or cell phone)

» Remote access to your office data including inventory, accounting, customer information any data you might need that's on your office computers (or in the cloud)

» Wireless connectivity (you want anytime access to your data)

» Security (ensure data going over the air is secure)

» Mobile applications (what tools will you use to be productive on the road)

Don't Buy Based on the Cool Factor

We are bombarded by new technology. Tech vendors are constantly marketing technology to us, to get us to buy it. Much of the technology is "cool"—it looks good. Furthermore, it seems like everyone else is buying it. If you buy technology to "keep up with the Joneses" and not based on a strategic technology plan and your current (or future) needs, you'll find yourself wasting money and time—and, frankly, become a bit frustrated.

Always remember: you don't need "cool," you need productivity. Of course there is nothing wrong with cool technology, but make sure that the cool technology is, first and foremost, right for you and your business and that it will boost your productivity and serve its purpose.

What Do You Do and Who are You?

Since there are so many different types of technology and with a dizzying array of options, it's best to really know WHAT you do and WHO you are. Your answers to these questions will determine what type of technology you should buy.

For example: if you only need to review occasional emails throughout the day, since you're in meetings a lot, you might not need to worry about a large screen for reviewing documents. Maybe you're an office manager and need to review and approve documents throughout the day. In this case, having a large screen and maybe even a keyboard is important to what you do and who you are.

Five Corners of Mobility

As you look to invest in a mobile solution, there are five corners of mobility you need to focus on:

1. Operating System
2. Hardware (form factor)
3. Security
4. Connectivity
5. Applications

Mobile Operating Systems

There are four main operating systems for smartphones: Apple's iPhone, Google's Android, Research in Motion's BlackBerry, and Windows Mobile (recently released Windows Phone 7).

Apple iPhone Platform

Apple's iPhone started the surge of interest in cool smartphones and their associated applications or "apps". Its phones have been the fastest selling phones for consumers and now corporate professionals are bringing it into their companies.

However, the demand of the iPhone is more than its hardware; it's all about the applications. The iPhone has had the most applications developed for it, although Google Android is growing. More and more independent developers, publishers, service providers (such as car rental companies, airlines, etc.) are developing new and improved applications for the iPhone.

Research In Motion's
BlackBerry

BlackBerry has been the leading platform for smartphones for mobile professionals. The BlackBerry is still regarded by many IT pros as among the most secure mobile device you can use. If you're in a highly regulated industry, the BlackBerry could be an option for you. Although BlackBerry does not have nearly the number of applications as the iPhone, especially for consumers, it does have a good number of applications for corporations, such as inventory and support and sales force automation software. BlackBerry has also pushed into making its platform more appealing to consumers.

Large companies love the BlackBerry as it is very secure and has remote management features. It's moved beyond just corporate offices. Solo professionals and consumers also like the BlackBerry for its simplicity and very powerful email functionality.

While BlackBerry does not have nearly the applications as the iPhone does, it is playing catch up with its own app store. Plus, there are many business-specific BlackBerry applications (the ones important to you). It's not the number of applications available overall that is important; it's knowing which types of apps are important and strategic to you and your business.

Google Android

Google's Android mobile operating system is the newest in the market.

The Android, possibly due to Google's heritage, is one of the more feature-rich phones. For example: it has HDMI ports for connecting to external monitors, and free GPS navigation.

All smart phones compete with each other, but the Android is probably a closer competitor to the iPhone than the Black-Berry—for now.

Since the devices have many similarities, sometimes it really does boil down to which apps you like best and which device supports them. Keep in mind that apps might not work the same on one device as they do on another device.

Google's Android is in direct competition with the iPhone and has built a strong developer base creating thousands of applications for it. It's increasing its market share and consumers and professionals are buying it.

Windows Mobile

With the 2010 release of Windows Phone 7, Windows has breathed new life into its mobile smartphone operating system, which so far has lagged behind Google Android and Apple iPhone in "coolness," applications and market share.

Microsoft Windows 7 phone offers a completely new interface. Those corporate users who want tight integration with Microsoft Office and the Windows platform will want to consider Windows 7. Users who are not happy with their current phones will want to try out Windows Phone 7 and see if the new interface is good for them.

Read this hands-on review of Windows Phone 7 here: http://smallbiztechnology.com/archive/2010/10/is-windows-phone-7-for-you-her.html

In Summary

The operating system you use is one of the most important decisions you'll make. It greatly affects your day to day use of the phone and can make your experience painful or joyful.

You also need to carefully select what wireless phone carrier you use. Maybe the phone carrier you choose does not have good reception in your city. Maybe another phone carrier does not have an option you might need, at a reasonable cost.

Smartphones are very important and possibly one of the most important tools your business uses. Choose your tool wisely.

Hardware

The hardware you purchase is very important and will be critical in determining how well you like your mobile device, how easy it is to use, and a variety of other factors.

Much of the decision of what hardware you buy will be based on the following variables:

- » Touch Screen vs. Physical Keyboard (for smartphones)
- » Large Screen vs. Small Screen
- » Flip Phone vs. Open Face (for smart phones)
- » Battery Life
- » Operating System
- » Carrier Availability

Notebook Computers

For many of you, a notebook computer is the basic component you need to access the Internet, write documents, and access files (and watch some movies) while away from the office. Although notebooks are a very mature market, with prices and types available for everyone, you still must ensure that you buy the right notebook for your needs.

Weight

You don't want a computer that is so heavy your back aches just by looking at it. But you also don't want one that is so thin and light that to type on it you need chop sticks to press the keyboard and a magnifying glass to read the monitor.

My ideal notebook is a 14" screen, 4lb notebook. Some professionals might want something even smaller, to more comfortably fit into their work bag. Some professionals may want a bigger screen and faster processor to do intensive computer work, such as video editing or graphic design.

Hard Disk Space

Your hard disk space needs to be as big as possible. Even though a lot of your work might be hosted on the Internet, when you download those 2GB videos and save those 50MB photos, you'll be glad your hard disk space is HUGE. Get nothing less than 200GB—much more if you can.

RAM
Memory is like money, you can never get enough of it. Get as much as you can. Common sizes are 2 – 4 Gigabytes. The more memory you have, the faster your software and applications will run.

Battery Life
Battery life is probably one of the most important concerns you should have when buying your notebook. If your battery only lasts 30 minutes and you have a two-hour client presentation, unplugged, you're going to be a bit uncomfortable as the clock moves to 28 minutes and counting. Get a long-life battery and ensure your notebook has power-saving features to help you get as much juice from your battery as possible.

Wireless
WiFi is a given on just about all notebooks. In addition to WiFi, many notebooks have options for built-in wireless broadband. This service offered by national cellular providers gives you wireless Internet access all around the country—on the train, on the bus, or in the back of a taxi without being connected to a local router like in the office or a coffee shop.

WiMax or 4G, a faster and longer reaching wireless protocol than WiFi is slowly emerging in the market. It is not widely available but expect more WiMax hot spots to be available, following a similar evolution of how WiFi grew.

Other things to consider

Many notebooks have built-in cameras for conducting videoconferences. Make sure you have sufficient amount of ports (USB, Firewire, PC Card / Express Card[1]) to connect all the devices you use with the notebook.

Netbooks

Netbooks are mini-computers, lighter and less powerful than notebook computers. Netbooks are an ideal compromise for executives who need a full-sized computer but don't want a notebook and find a smartphone not sufficient.

These $500 (or so) devices are a little bigger than a paperback book and are ideal for light computing needs. I find that the screens are way too small for all-day computing, but can be useful for a few hours of email and document writing. The keyboards are quite small but do have an "acquired taste" after a few hours of use.

Smartphones

Smartphones are definitely a tool every mobile professional needs. The key is choosing what's best for you. There are dozens of different handset vendors and wireless carriers. When deciding which smartphone is best for you, you need to know what YOU do and how this tool can enhance your productivity. If you're like me and you only need a phone to speak on and check email, then you can make do with a very simple phone that is perfect for these tasks. If, however, you want to manage your business on your phone, a phone with a large screen and the ability to run a variety of business applications is something that you may need to consider.

Tablet Computing

Tablet computing platforms have gone up and down in popularity. Many PC vendors have produced variations of Tablet computers over the years. Recently, Apple released an iPhone-based iPad which has caused a resurgence in the "tablet" computer world. Samsung and other vendors have released Android-based tablets.

---

1 http://en.wikipedia.org/wiki/Express_Card

Mobile Security

Ensure that your mobile computing experience is secure. Some basic steps for securing your data are as follows:

The connection to the Internet or another network should be secure. When computing on the road, you often can't control your access to the Internet. You don't know who the Internet Service Provider is, whose server your data is going through, or if the WiFi hotspot you are connecting to is even authentic. Using a virtual private network (VPN), especially for very sensitive information, will ensure that all the data that leave your computer (or smartphone) are encrypted.

> **Ensure that when you type your password, other eyes (like the guy next to you on the train) are not observing you. Also use difficult passwords, combined with letters and numbers and a mixture of cases."**

HOT TIP: Talk to your local IT consultant to help you setup a VPN. Check out this link for more information on a VPN:
http://searchcio_midmarket.techtarget.com/sDefinition/0,,sid183_gci995953,00.html

Ensure that when you type your password, other eyes (like the guy next to you on the train) are not observing you. Also use difficult passwords, combined with letters and numbers and a mixture of cases.

Encrypt your data so that if your notebook computer or smartphone is lost or stolen, the data cannot be accessed.

Back up your data so that you can recover your data if your mobile device is lost or stolen.

If you store as little information as possible on your mobile device, you won't have to worry about the data that's not there ever being accessed by unauthorized users. Of course you'll still have to worry about the data that goes over the Internet (email attachments, web sites) or via external devices (like USB thumb drives).

Keep in mind that for smartphones, some devices are more secure than others as they have more built-in security measures, encryption, and remote management options available to them.

Among the iPhone, Android, BlackBerry, and Windows Phone 7 operating systems, most professionals will agree that the Black-Berry and Windows Mobile operating systems are the most secure.

Overall the POLICIES you implement for yourself and for mobile users are going to be your best line of defense. For example: before smartphones or notebooks connect to your network, are they scanned? Do you limit what web sites mobile users can access? Have you trained your staff in how to be safe online?

Wireless Carrier

Your cell phone is useless if you can't call someone. If you bought a cell phone to check your email and there's limited service, then you won't be checking too many emails.

The cell phone carrier you choose is so important.

Here are two things you want consider when choosing a cell phone carrier:

» Customer service: When something goes wrong (i.e. you're charged too much, lose your phone or need to add a new line), you want to ensure that the carrier is there to help you.

» Cell Network: If you are on the road for much of the day, it's pointless to have a carrier whose cell phone signal is often spotty wherever you go. Ensure that your cell phone signal is strong and that your voice is clear. Don't just search for a cell phone carrier based on the monthly fees.

Connectivity

When on the road it is important that you can access the data in your office. There are several ways you can do this:

Store data on online services such as Dropbox, Box.net, WebOffice, HyperOffice, Egnyte, Google Apps, or Microsoft SkyDrive. These documents don't reside on the server in your office; they reside on hosted servers and are accessed through the Internet.

Another option is to have your files on a server(s) in your office and remotely access data on your server via a "virtual private network"[2] (VPN). A VPN is a way to securely access files on your office server, through an encrypted connection.

A third option is to store files in your desktop computer and access them through remote control (remote access) through

---

2 http://en.wikipedia.org/wiki/Virtual_private_network

software from PC Anywhere, GoToMyPC, TeamViewer, LapLink, or other similar remote access services and software.

You might find that a hybrid connectivity option wherein you access some files on a commercial service, like Dropbox, and access other files remotely on your local server is best for your situation.

Applications

Applications are the POWER that make your smartphone (or notebook computers) work. For notebook computers, I won't go into what applications you should or should not have. These are the same, or similar, applications you have on your desktop computer.

For smartphones, there are thousands of applications that software developers make for your enjoyment, productivity, and yes, business use. Some applications are free and some are fee-based but most cost under $3 to use.

Get recommendations from your peers to find the best mobile software and, in particular, smartphone applications. Second, review your day-to-day responsibilities and business processes and see what mobile applications can be downloaded to make these processes and responsibilities much easier. Third, review your existing software and see if the software vendor or hosted application provider has an accompanying app for their software or hosted application.

(

Mobile Computing Resources

Walt Mossberg's Notebook Computer Buying Guide
http://ptech.allthingsd.com/20080410/consider-your-needs-then-use-this-guide-to-buying-a-laptop/

Do More With Your Smartphone: Five Cool Tools for Your Smart Phone
http://www.nyreport.com/index.cfm?fuseaction=Feature.showFeature&FeatureID=778

The Mobile Office
http://smallbusiness.intuit.com/blog/where-small-is-now/2010/04/the-mobile-office.html

Security 101: An Executive Guide to Mobile Security
http://www.cio.com.au/article/268162/mobile_security_101_an_executive_guide_mobile_security/?

Watch Ramon's interview with Revision 3 about mobile solutions for your business here:
http://revision3.com/hpinsight02

Watch Ramon's 60-minute webinar with Intuit, all about how to manage your business just as well out of the office as in the office.
http://community.intuit.com/events/the-mobile-office-w-ramon-ray-productivity-anywhere

CHAPTER 4:
Customer Relationship Management (CRM)

What is It? Customer relationship management (CRM) is the process wherein businesses can learn about their customers' preference, service needs, and buying habits and use this information to sell more to the customer, sell different products to the customer, or serve the customer better.

good CRM system will help develop loyal customers, nurture new customers, and overall boost profits and revenues.

CRM is not a contact database. A contact management system is simply a list of customer names and contact information; it might even have some customer preferences or profiles. But it's still not CRM.

CRM is much more. It's about knowing what customers have purchased. Know (or better predict) what they will buy in the future. Know what they like and don't like.

Automation

Good CRM tools will also help to automate things. For example, if a customer buys five pairs of socks in three days, you might configure your CRM program to offer them a sixth pair of socks for free. Or maybe if a customer downloads an ebook about how to buy gifts for babies, it will automatically add them to your database about how to feed babies.

One part of CRM is the tool used to store customer information. A second part enables you to actually serve customers better by predicting what they'll buy and proposing targeted offerings to segments of customers. A third, key part of CRM is your ability to use the tool.

Amazon.com is a good example of CRM in action! The more you purchase from Amazon.com, the more it knows what you like. Amazon.com's technology helps you shop by telling you what others purchased, who bought what you bought. Another example of CRM in action is Proflowers.com. When you buy flowers you are prompted to enter one (or more) person's birthday. A few days before their birthday you are emailed by Proflowers.com and prompted to order flowers for them.

CRM Is Simple: Know Your Customers

CRM is not "one particular" process or technology. It's a system, often an integration of several different systems that enhance the buying experience for customers and increase revenues and profits for the company.

Small businesses can implement very simple CRM systems, it's not only for larger companies.

Smallbizcrm.com writes that if you have some of these questions CRM is something you need to consider.

» Why did you lose that deal?
» Just when did you promise to get back to ACME Inc.? After their budget gets approved?
» Exactly how much did you quote them?
» Who from your sales/service or accounts departments last engaged with that client? When and what transpired?
» What is the weighted value of those potential deals, forecast for the next X months?
» You have a great, new deal sweetener and need to get a mailer, fax shot, emailer out to your clients in a hurry, but how?
» Who are your VIP customers, by region, product, rep, or any other user-defined category? How do you rate or profile them?
» You can't pinpoint just why Johnny is having problems closing deals.

» You want to sell your business but you can't show your prospective buyers a professional, current list of your pending deals or active clients, the goodwill that makes much of the real value of any business.

Check out their full article on CRM here: http://www.small-bizcrm.com/does-your-small-business-need-a-software-solution. html

Here's a short list of CRM solutions you might want to consider:

» Infusion Soft - http://www.infusionsoft.com
» NetSuite - http://www.netsuite.com
» BatchBlue - http://www.batchblue.com
» SalesLogix - http://www.saleslogix.com

Traditional CRM vs. Social CRM
From http://technology.inc.com/software/articles/200906/leary. html (used with permission) by Brent Leary

Traditional customer relationship management's strong suit has been improved operational effectiveness, easier access to data, and improved collaboration. Social media adds the dimension of connecting with potential customers.

Connecting with potential customers is one of the biggest challenges facing small businesses today. A recent study by Network Solutions and the University of Maryland shows that marketing/innovation is the single biggest competitive disadvantage confronting small business, after access to capital. In fact, converting marketing leads into buyers and finding efficient ways to promote and advertise, are two areas small businesses say they struggle the most with. This finding is supported by a recent Microsoft small business study, which found customer acquisition and retention to be the biggest challenges facing their small business partners.

To help overcome customer acquisition challenges, many small businesses are looking into customer relationship management (CRM) tools and strategies. In the past, many viewed CRM as being too complex and expensive to implement for the expected return on investment. But over the last couple of years, software-as-a-service (SaaS) offerings from the likes of Salesforce.com, NetSuite, and a host of others have allowed companies of all sizes to implement CRM products and services at a fraction of the cost, time, and effort needed in the past.

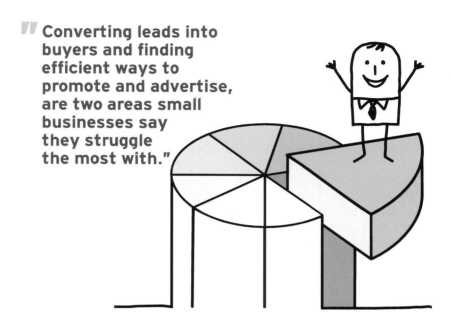

" Converting leads into buyers and finding efficient ways to promote and advertise, are two areas small businesses say they struggle the most with."

Traditionally, CRM's strong suit has been improved operational effectiveness, easier access to information, and improved interdepartmental collaboration. While these are critically important to the success of any business, the focal point of these areas is internal to the company. And while a more efficient company should have a positive impact on customer interaction and responsiveness, does it really help us to meaningfully connect with those potential customers empowered in a Web 2.0 world?

Social media adds this missing dimension to the traditional, operational areas of CRM. And according to a recent Nielsen Company study, two-thirds of the world's Internet population visited a social networking site or blogging site—what they refer to as "member communities." The integration of social media into CRM strategy—called Social CRM—differs in focus from traditional customer relationship management in a few key ways.

Data-driven vs. Content-driven

Businesses began investing in CRM applications in the '90s mainly to store contact data. Before contact management software was available, businesses had to store their valuable customer information in Rolodexes, spreadsheets, and even filing cabinets.

It was important to have a central location to store the data that was also easily accessible to communicate effectively with contacts. And with multiple people "touching" the customer for various reasons, it quickly became important to be able to track activities, appointments, potential deals, notes, and other information. Consequently, traditional CRM grew out of this need to store, track, and report on critical information about customers and prospects.

Social CRM is growing out of a completely different need—the need to attract the attention of those using the Internet to find answers to business challenges they are trying to overcome. And nothing captivates the attention of searchers like relevant, compelling content. Having the right content, and enough of it, will help connect you with those needing your product or service. Creating content in formats that make it easy for your target audience to consume it increases the probability that you will move them to action—starting a conversation with you. Whether it's by developing a blog post, podcast, YouTube video, or Webinar, creating attractive content is a key pillar of social CRM strategy.

Process-centric vs. Conversation-centric

Traditional customer relationship management is heavily focused on implementing and automating processes. Companies looking to implement processes like lead and activity management would turn to CRM. Management would turn to CRM to standardize on sales processes to increase the accuracy of sales forecasts. And customer service requests could be tracked, routed, escalated, and resolved in a uniform fashion to ensure proper handling. Traditional CRM helped make it possible to ensure the proper activities and tasks would be performed by the appropriate people, in the correct sequences.

While there are processes involved in building a successful social CRM strategy, conversations are at the heart of it. Having meaningful conversations with those searching for the help you can provide is the turning point in transforming clicks into customers. The processes involved are aimed at making it easy for people to find us (through our content) and invite us into a conversation—on their terms. This may take the form of a comment left on a blog post, following your company on Twitter, or possibly embedding your PowerPoint presentation on their webpage. There are numerous ways to participate in meaningful conversations with people looking for help in solving challenges. Formalizing a strategy to increase the likelihood of engaging in these conversations is a tenant of social CRM.

Operationally-focused vs. People/Community-focused

As mentioned above, managing customer information is a major concern to businesses of all sizes. It plays a key role in the ability of businesses to respond to customer requests, manage resources needed to close deals efficiently, and provide management with reports to keep track of sales performance. This helps executives achieve operational effectiveness, and is particularly important for businesses expanding their sales and marketing operations, needing to implement new processes to manage growth. Businesses have typically turned to CRM to improve communication between sales and marketing operations, as well as to improve data-access to positively impact decision making.

Whereas traditional CRM activity focused heavily on operational effectiveness and its impact—both internally and on the customer—social CRM is all about people and community. It's about how your company intends to participate in the ongoing conversations taking place in the industry. How you embrace non-traditional influential people like popular industry bloggers and social sites on the Web frequented by your audience. And fully understanding the importance of contributing to discussions, in a transparent manner, will help you build the kind of reputation needed to become a valued member of the online communities important to your business.

So if you're turning to CRM to help bring in new customers, you'll have to go beyond traditional CRM focuses by integrating social media-infused tactics and strategies. But it's important to remember social CRM is not a substitute, but a much needed complement to traditional areas of customer relationship management. It gets us close to what we've needed all along.

A small-business technology analyst, adviser, and award-winning blogger, Brent Leary is the co-author of Barack 2.0: Social Media Lessons for Small Business. His blog can be found at http://brentleary.com, or follow him on Twitter at http://twitter.com/brentleary.

CRM Resources

Destination CRM
http://www.destinationcrm.com/
Articles/CRM-News/Daily-News/What-
Is-CRM-46033.aspx

**Social CRM: Not Your Father's Cus-
tomer Relationship Management**
http://smallbiztrends.
com/2008/05/social-crm.html

**5 Reasons Why CRM is Even More
Important During a Recession**
http://www.insidecrm.com/features/
crm-important-recession-082508/

What is CRM
http://www.insidecrm.com/blog/what-
is-crm-2.php#more-151

CHAPTER 5:
Protecting Your Data

Securing your company's data is a very important part in ensuring the viability and integrity of your company. Security is like insurance or a floatation vest; you only see the need for it when something unfortunate happens. It's one of those items on business "to do lists" that many small businesses tend to easily forget. It doesn't even generate revenue, so that's another reason it's often relegated to the back burner by so many.

What are some aspects of data security you need to consider?

When thinking of data security think of all the entry points to your data where a hacker or otherwise unauthorized person might have access.

This includes your network, desktop computers, mobile technologies (notebook and smartphone), and web site. It might very well also include your telephone system and hosted applications.

Work with a security expert (a local one or with a company that provides this as service) to ensure your company is as secure as possible.

The best place to start when you're looking for a security expert is your IT consultant. A seasoned IT consultant should have the expertise to properly secure your computers and networks. If they do not, check with your security software vendor, such as Symantec, Trend Micro, McAfee and others, to see who they recommend. In fact, many of these vendors have resellers who are security experts.

Every business should have a basic level of information security protection. However, some businesses, due to their vulnerability or attraction to malicious persons, might need more security. If you are selling nuclear missiles to the federal government, your security needs to be more secure than your neighbor selling coffee to local commuters.

What Needs to be Secured?

Email

Ensuring email you receive and send, including attachments, is secure is critical. Both incoming and outgoing email must be virus- and malware-free.

Network

Your network needs to be secure from outside attacks, and it is important that you have systems in place (such as a firewall, router, or other) to ensure data that should NOT leave (or enter) the network does not do so. You need to also ensure that unauthorized users do not have access to the network. Your servers, part of your network, are also part of this equation and need to be protected.

TIP: It's important to configure your network so that it is not only protected from outside attack (hackers) but also attack from the inside, hence the term "unauthorized users," be they employees or criminals.

Desktop and Notebook Computer

Each of your desktop and notebook computers needs to have an anti-virus program installed, at a bare minimum. Web browsers also need to be secured so that end users don't inadvertently access sites designed to steal data or infect computers.

Many security softwares have built-in web filtering technology to check for links and web sites that might have malicious code. You can also install web filtering and monitoring software that blocks web sites that have "objectionable" content or web sites that are known hacker sites.

Mobile Devices

Your mobile devices need to be protected to ensure that if they are lost, the data is encrypted and can't be read by unauthorized users. Since smartphones are in fact computers, consider anti-virus and other added software to enhance security as well. Also bear in mind that your mobile devices, including smart-phones are often gateways to your network, so ensuring they are secure is even more important.

If all of your data are accessed and stored on a remote server, there's no concern about your mobile data falling into the wrong hands if your device is lost or stolen. However, if you store data on your cell phone, consider encrypting the informa-tion with third party software made for mobile phone encryption.

Password protecting your phone will also deter hackers from accessing your data if they get access to your phone.

Web Site

Ensuring your web site is secure is VERY important but often ignored. A hacker accessing your customers' credit card records or personal information is just as dangerous as one who has hacked your network and has access to your inventory database or contracts on a corporate server. It's best to NOT host your web site yourself on your own servers, but to let your web site be hosted by a web host. They are using professionals to ensure your data is safe and backed up and this is all they do, protect your (and others') web sites.

If you are hosting your web site on your own servers, con-sult with a security expert to ensure it is as secure as possible. Keep in mind that if a hacker gains entry to your web site, they might also be able to access your network through your web site, as your web site, in many cases, is simply an extension of your network.

If you are creating customized applications for your web site, ensure that these applications are properly designed so that hackers do not have a known or unknown backdoor to ac-cess the application.

Data Security Tools
The Human Mind

"Social engineering" attacks are on the rise, and you must edu-cate your employees, customers, partners.

"Social engineering" attacks are attacks by hackers wherein they access your information not by technologically hacking your computer system. Instead they "sweet talk" someone into giving them all or some of the information they need to hack into your computer system.

In Kevin Mitnick's book, "The Art of Deception," he writes how many of these security breaches were successfully done, not by using technology, but by getting the right person within a company to give him the information he needed (used by itself or in combination with other information), such as passwords, account numbers, user names, etc. By "sweet talking" an unsuspecting secretary, for example, he could make her think he was in the IT department of her company and needed her password for some technical reason. Alert your employees to NEVER give out their user name, password, or any other details unless they are absolutely certain who they are giving it to. Many companies have policies that passwords, for example, should NEVER be given out to anyone.

Firewalls

Firewalls are one of the first lines of defense for your network and individual computers. Their job is to ensure that only information you authorize leaves and enters your computer system. Hardware firewalls are physical appliances that should be installed on the outer perimeter of your network. You want to ensure that they serve as the first line of defense to protect your network. Software firewalls should be installed in every computer. Firewalls can't be simply installed right out of the box. They should be properly configured by a security expert to make sure they are optimized for the best security for your business.

❞Think what would happen if you came into your office tomorrow and realized all your data as erased. Would that be a problem? For many businesses this would lead them out of business."

Anti-Virus Software

Viruses will attack your computer. Anti-virus is a MUST to ensure that viruses do not cripple your computers. The question is not "WILL you be sent a virus?" but "WHEN a virus comes (and you might get sent many viruses per day attached to spam messages), do you have the tools to block the virus and prevent it from infecting your computer system?" Viruses should not be your only concern; online scams such as phishing, to get you to inadvertently think you are accessing your bank account when you are actually accessing a hacker's web site that LOOKS like your bank, is also of great concern. Many anti-virus products are bundled with anti-phishing and other security features.

Intrusion Detection Systems (IDS)

These systems add a third layer of security to your network and help ensure that malicious activity that was not blocked or detected by your firewall or anti-virus product is stopped before it damages your business. Some viruses, for example, are programmed so well by their creators that they appear to be legitimate traffic that should be allowed to go through your network. In reality they are software that can bring down your entire network. In this case an IDS will do its best to detect activity that could be a threat to your network.

Backing Up Your Data

One of the big reasons many companies go out of business after a disaster is due to lack of data to re-start the business.

Many of us who do backup our data probably are not doing it enough or are doing it incorrectly. Close your eyes and think what would happen if you came into your office tomorrow and realized all your data as erased. Would that be a problem? For many businesses this would lead them out of business. Backing up your data ensures that when data is lost, you can recover it. Backup solutions include backing up data to an online storage service, to a CD, or some other removable media or even to another computer or hard disk. Whichever method you choose, make sure you test the backup. What a shame it would be to backup data year after year, and realize that when you need it, the data was not really being backed up or the backed up data is corrupted and not usable!

Application Security
The security of your online applications (or custom software) is not talked about as much as viruses or phishing, but it is an equally important aspect of your total security solution. Maybe you sell shoes via a web site and use an online database to handle the customer information and ecommerce transactions. If the program itself is not secure, maybe there is a "back door" security vulnerability that your programmer did not know about. A hacker can exploit it to steal information. As you run your business using online applications or even applications on an internal computer network, you must ensure that the application is secure and that unauthorized users do not have access to it.

Wireless Security
When your business is computing in a mobile world, wireless security must be at the top of your mind. As your sales people in Maine are using a wireless Internet connection, a hacker is snatching their data from the air and stealing their credit card numbers. Is your competition wirelessly accessing your network and downloading your customer records and quarterly sales data? It is important that the data in your mobile device is encrypted and password-protected. Work with your wireless service provider to ensure your wireless connection to the Internet is secure. When you access your corporate network (wirelessly or wired), use a virtual private network (VPN) to ensure data transmissions are secure.

You also want to ensure that access to your wireless network is secure and that all access points and related wireless access mechanisms are properly configured to be as secure as possible.

Web Monitoring
I received a press release saying that, according to the Fantasy Sports Trade Association (FSTA), more than 14 million people are playing Fantasy Football. According to outplacement consultants Challenger, Gray & Christmas, during the National Football League regular season, nearly 37 million people spend an average of 50 minutes a week at work managing their fantasy teams. John Challenger, CEO of the consulting firm, states fantasy sport ranks alongside shopping on eBay's web auction site and online poker as the biggest waste of productivity at the workplace. What does this mean for your business?

Instead of calling customers, preparing invoices, writing up reports, or taking supplemental online training, your employees are busy doing their own online work—but not yours. Having insight into what your employees are doing online is important. It's not a matter of "spying" on them, but it's a matter of ensuring they are productive.

Consider implementing software to manage and monitor the web activities of your employees.

Your Own Employees as the First Line of Defense

Remember, you can have all the hi-tech security gadgets in the world, but if your employee is writing their user name and passwords down on a sticky note on their computer, you've just had a huge hole shot through your security net!

Backup and Recovery 101

(First appeared on Symantec's web site at http://www.symantec.com/business/solutions/article.jsp?aid=20091117_backup_101)

Security is not complete without security against malware, hackers, viruses, etc—AND ALSO a complete backup and recovery solution.

More than Files: Applications and Operating System Too

Maybe you do have a backup solution in place for files and data you and/or your employees create. Maybe your file server is backed up, for example. But what if your file server hard disk fails? What if an employee's computer fails? Restoring the files is only one part of the equation. You need to ensure the applications and operating system can also be quickly restored. For example: most business professionals use Microsoft Outlook. You might be able to reinstall Outlook in your computer, but if your data is not backed up, you won't have your email, your calendar, your task list, or anything. Work with a technology professional to ensure that files, applications, and operating systems are backed up as well. Discuss with them about creating an "image" of your servers and client computers.

Don't Forget Mobile Workers

We live in an increasingly mobile society where business data no longer only resides in local servers in a dusty filing closet. It doesn't only reside in desktop computers in cubicles or a CEO's oak executive desk. Today's professionals create their data and store their data in a variety of mobile devices: smartphones, netbooks, notebooks, and USB keys.

The $100,000 client contract might have originally been created in the corporate office. But maybe the remote sales staff did the final and most critical edits on a smart phone at the airport.

It is important that your backup strategy includes ALL of your corporate data, whether it is in the office our outside of the office.

Where Will You Back Up Your Data

You have several choices in deciding where to back up your data. In fact you don't have to have one option, but you might decide to implement two solutions.

Backing up your data to another hard disk, server, or removable media (such as a DVD) is a great option, especially when you want to ensure quick access to the data. The backed up data should not be stored in your office, but should be taken offsite (like to an employee's home). In the event something happens to your office (fire, flood, earthquake, theft), your data is safe and easily recoverable. Taking your data "home" does not mean you want to leave it on the kitchen table to be dropped in the dish water. Store it in a file cabinet, or any other safe and secure location.

Online backup is a great option if you want a hassle-free way to ensure your data is automatically backed up, remotely archived, and accessible through the Internet for recovery. The challenge with this solution, however, is that recovery of your data must be done by downloading your files through the Internet (unless the online backup company can send you DVDs of your data). Although recovering files you created is not hard using an online backup solution, recovering your programs, operating systems, and data files can be a challenge.

Verify Your Backup

It is absolutely critical that you ensure your data is being properly backed up.

Imagine depositing your money into an ATM machine, only to realize that when you want to make a withdrawal, the money you were depositing was not applied to your bank account. To ensure your bank account is properly credited, get a receipt and check your bank balances after a few days to ensure the money has been properly deposited.

When backing up your data, it is absolutely critical to ensure that the data has been actually backed up. Backing up 6 months of data is great. But if disaster strikes in 6 months plus one day and only then do you realize that your data has not been properly backed up, then it is too late.

Technology can fail and human error is commonplace. Maybe you thought your three servers and 20 computers were backed up every night, but instead only two servers were backed up. Double check and verify that what you want to back up is indeed being backed up. Look at the backup logs or alerts on failed jobs but also spot-check the actual backed up data.

Data Recovery

Data recovery is something that no business wants to have to do. However, knowing how to do it is essential. The data recovery process will differ from system to system, but overall the principle is the same. In fact, I encourage you to do practice "data recovery drills" to measure the effectiveness of your data recovery process.

If you need to recover files, and your computer is operational, simply access your backup software, access the recovery feature, and select which files you need to recover.

If your entire computer or server goes down, this is where your "image" comes into play.

Start up your computer from an external drive, like a USB drive or DVD drive. Start up the software that manages your backup and/or image. Select the backed up image you would like to restore to the new computer hard disk. Once the recovery process is done, you'll have a computer identical to your "old" or crashed computer. All you have to do now is install any programs or files that were newly installed since the image was created.

Disaster Continuity

As you put together a backup plan, it's important to consider disaster continuity. This means that in the event of a disaster your business can continue running as effectively as possible. Here are a few things to consider including in your plan:

- » Telephone numbers: Do you have complete contact details of all your key employees and ALL staff? And maybe your IT partner or consultant?
- » Customer information: Can you easily find complete contact information for all of your customers?

» Central communication: Does everyone in the company have a central telephone number, web site, and/or point of contact for sharing information?

» Remote office: In the event you are unable to access your office, can you and your employees remotely access company information?

While you can't control whether disaster will strike, you can control whether the impact it has on your business will be devastating or merely inconvenient. Make sure that you are implementing a system of protection that includes regular backup of files (local and remote) and operating systems, a sensible backup location, regular verification that it's actually backing up, recovery "practice" sessions, and a continuity plan that all key employees know about. It can mean the difference between staying in business or not.

Protecting Your Data Resources

Anti Virus, MalWare and Other Security Products
Symantec - http://www.symantec.com, McAfee - http://www.mcafee.com, TrendMicro - http://www.trendmicro.com, AVG http://www.avg.com (free version and fee based)

5 Biggest Social Media Security Risks for Small Businesses (Fast Company Magazine)
http://www.fastcompany.com/1563867/the-5-biggest-social-media-security-risks-for-businesses

The Security Risks of Social Networks (Focus)
http://www.focus.com/fyi/it-security/security-risks-social-networks/

Microsoft Computer Security
http://www.microsoft.com/security/default.aspx

CHAPTER 6:
Building Business Class Web Sites

Most of you reading this already have web sites; in fact many of you probably have great-looking web sites with advanced functionality. However for the many of you without one or with a web site that is not being used to its maximum advantage, let's talk about (re)building business class web sites.

Social media (as in Blogs, Facebook, etc.) is VERY important to the online communication and marketing dimensions of your business. However, I still do think that a VERY well-designed web site is very important for every business to have.

I wrote "Building Business Class Web Sites: 10 Musts"[3] around 2004, but guess what? The information is STILL relevant today.

10 things you MUST consider when building a business class web site:

1. Focus on the customer
2. Have a plan
3. Easy to remember name
4. Easy navigation
5. Informative
6. Security
7. Easy customer contact
8. Fresh content
9. Be found
10. Be simple - KIS

Focus on the customer

It's so easy to get caught up in the excitement of building your web site that you FORGET ABOUT YOUR CUSTOMERS. However, as you're building your web site, keep them in the forefront of your mind. Focus on the audience that will be using your web site. If it's an intranet for internal corporate use, then your "customers" are going to be the employees and/or business partners using the web site. If it's a public web site for your business customers, then ensure that their needs are at the top of your priority list.

As children, you probably learned about the "me, me, me, me, me, me, me, me, me" song. No one likes to be around a "me"-centered person. However, those who share, who give, who look out for the needs of others will always be in high demand.

A client who owned a limousine company came to me one day and wanted a web site for his business. After talking for a few days, he brought me several photographs of his limousine that he wanted on the front page of his web site.

---

3 http://smallbiztechnology.com/10websitemusts/

He was not customer-focused but only thinking of his pride and joy: his limousine. I suggested that instead of filling the first page of this web site with a picture of his limousine, he first consider the most important things customers want when they contact him. Is there a car available? How much does it cost to go from point A to point B? How long will it take? Etc.

Build a web site focused on your customers and you can only succeed. Build a web site focused on yourself and you'll fail.

One thing I did in the beginning stages of smallbiztechnology.com's development was to post the following, in fairly large type: "Do you like or hate this web site?" Guess what? Over the months, I got dozens and dozens of opinions on how I could make my web site much better—and what I had been doing right.

TIP: web site traffic analysis tool. I use Google Analytics to analyze traffic coming to smallbiztechnology.com. I can see how many visitors have been to my web site, which web sites referred them, what type of web browser they use, and a lot more stats. with this information, I can customize my web site according to my visitors and make better decisions on smallbiztechnology.com's development.

Have a Plan

Building a web site is no different from going on a journey. You're starting somewhere and you want to get somewhere. The only way you are going to get there is with a plan—or road map.

Before you even put the first dot in dot-com, sit down and think. Ask yourself:

» Why do I want a web site?
» What is it going to accomplish?
» What is the benefit to my business and customers?

Choosing a Name

How many times have you heard a radio advertisement, or seen a television advertisement for a web site with a hard to remember name?

In all of my speeches and presentations, I drive home the importance of having an easy to remember name to my audience.

One huge no-no: DO NOT use hyphens in your web site name, they are too hard to remember to put them in. And when saying them to people, or even in an ad, they get in the way of saying a simple name.

Another web site name no, no: Let's say your business is Fuddleston Fisherie. If your business is not a household name, or even if it is, make sure your web site is not fuddlestonfisherie.com!

It's much easier to remember qualityfish.com or something similar than a web site with your name—if it's one like Fuddleston Fisherie.

One suggestion you might wish to consider is having two web site names. One can be your long and hard to spell brand or corporate name and one can be a much simpler version.

Both web site addresses can point to the same web site, so you won't have to update two different web sites.

Make Navigation Easy

Sometimes you visit a web site and it makes you seasick. You regret going to the site. You get so confused your head starts pounding.

Is your site like this?

Do you make it easy for users of your web site to find the information they need? Do you make it easy for them to find the information YOU want them to find?

"Do you make it easy for users of your web site to find the information they need? Do you make it easy for them to find the information YOU want them to find?"

I've been to web sites where the "buy" button is almost hidden. Think of going to a physical retail store and the cash register is hidden!

Remember: your web site is only one of many others selling the same things. Whether you're selling goods or services, your competition is only a mouse click away.

When people visit your web site, make sure they can clearly and very easily find the information they need. You don't want to be too simplistic and have only two web links per page. But you don't want to be overly complex and force your web site visitors to use a map just to navigate your web site.

Sure, every user is not going to instantly find everything they need on your web site and that's where a good search engine for your web site—and web site directory—come into play. But do not lean on these tools as a crutch or excuse for poor web site design!

If you have a very simple web site with only a few pages, there's no excuse for all the information you have to not be easily accessible. If you have thousands and thousands of pages of information, your goal should be to categorize the information in a logical layout, provide top level navigation to the main sections of your site and, if needed, use sub-sections. Then supplement this with a good search engine and web site directory.

Make It Informative

If you are going to promote your web site as a news site, or portal of knowledge, then make sure your site is informative.

Remember those mornings when you crave for a bowl of cereal? My favorite is Wheat Chex. You reach for the cereal, pour it in the bowl...only to have three pieces of cereal come out!

It's disappointing. It's frustrating. It leaves a bad taste in your mouth.

Building an information-rich web site takes a lot of time and energy. But the rewards can be immense. Over time you'll find that your web site (and your company) will become known as a resource. The next logical progression, if you work at it is that a) customers will want to purchase their goods and services from you—you ARE the expert, right? b) the press will call you, asking for your insight on various topics—free press!

A great tool to use for easily updating your web site with journal-like information is a blog. A blog is one of the best tools you can use for continuously updated information. Items you post to your web site are automatically tagged with a date, time, and the name of the user who posted it. Your blogging tool will also archive your blogs for you automatically. More on this later.

Security

As I tell the audience at my seminars, your web site has to be as secure as the information it stores.

If your web site is going to be storing credit card numbers, personal information, customer lists, etc, you should invest in the security of your web site, commensurate with the value of that data and your business.

Businesses running a $50,000-a-year web site should not go into debt and purchase a $75,000-per-year security solution.

If your web server is connected to your corporate network(s), the security of your web site is even that more important. If a hacker can get access to your web server, it's only a matter of time before they can find a way through it to a computer on your network. It's best to ensure your web site is NOT connected to your computer network.

However, YOU are ultimately responsible for your own web site's security. Remember: if you install a script, put up a database or some other web application and it has security holes (even just one), there's nothing your web host or e-commerce provider can do about it.

Easy Customer Contact

One of the most frustrating experiences in visiting a web site is not being able to communicate with the web site owners (be it sales, customer service, etc.) about a question (or comment) you have.

Successful vendors such as PC Mall, CDW, Amazon.com, and many others have clearly labeled "contact points" on their web sites. Some have an 800 number clearly displayed on every page of their web site. Some encourage you to email them or use a web form. But either way, a contact method is provided.

Analyze your own web site. What image are you portraying?

Do you solicit a customer's business online, only to slap them in the face by not making contact information clearly visible or making it not available at all?

One of the easiest contact methods is to create a web form that will enable your customers to send you a message via your web site. The next step, which many more businesses fail at, is to respond in a timely fashion to your customers.

I've gotten emails from some companies saying, "thanks for your message, we'll be sure to contact you in 24 - 72 hours." In this day and age, where your web site is only a click away from a competitor's, a 24-hour response time is the minimum.

Instead:

» Every message that comes in should be automatically responded to so the sender knows you have received the message. How many times have you heard, from your own friends and colleagues, "I didn't get your email." Well sometimes maybe they are lying but sometimes email messages simply don't get through.

» The next step is to ensure that someone personally replies to your customer's message with an answer.

If your inbound communication is not that much, then you can handle the inbound email in a more or less manual fashion. However, as your business grows, you should look into a commercial customer support (email or web form) management solution.

Another dimension to online support is live chat. Companies such as Live Person enable customers to initiate chat sessions, directly from your web site, for instant communication.

Igo.com successfully uses this feature on their web site; hence, I'm a repeat customer. The only caveat about these live chat services is that businesses like to display that "chat with an operator now" button, but oftentimes I've been disappointed to see that there's a "no operator available" sign after clicking on the button.

Keep It Fresh

No one likes stale bread, cereal or milk—and your web site is not different. When visitors come to your web site, it's an added bonus when they see fresh information. Show me a web site built in 2001. If that web site has not changed one bit in 2003, I'm not so sure if I want to do business with them. Maybe they, like their web site, are "dead"—or close to it.

If your web site is going to display news of any kind or serve as a "portal," it is even more important that the content you display is fresh, ESPECIALLY if you have dates next to the content!

One of the ways to keep your web site fresh is to integrate your blog, email newsletter, and social media updates with your web site. Every time you post a new blog post, send out an email newsletter or update one of your social media accounts. This should be reflected on your web site.

Be Found

Just because you have a web site does not mean that anyone but yourself, your web developer, and your mother will know about it. Once your web site is built, you've got to market it and let the world know about it. YOUR world may be your customers. If you have a service or retail base of existing customers, don't waste money advertising your web site around the world. FIRST market your web site to your current customers and let them know that it's there and all the things they can do with it. Once that's done, as necessary, you can then start marketing your web site to new customers and prospects.

Be Simple – KIS (Keep It Simple)

Last but not least: as you build your web site, think with simplicity in mind. Don't try to cram the whole universe and everything about your business into it.

"No one likes stale bread, cereal or milk and your web site is not different. When visitors come to your web site, it's an added bonus when they see fresh information."

Building Business Class Web Sites Resources

Intuit Website Services
http://www.intuit.com/website-building-software/

WordPress.com

Yahoo
http://webhosting.yahoo.com

Network Solutions
http://www.networksolutions.com

Jimdo
http://www.jimdo.com

Web.com

CHAPTER 7:
Online Marketing & Advertising

The beauty of marketing on the Internet, as opposed to more traditional marketing—such as on the side of a blimp, radio advertising, print advertising, billboard advertising, or television advertising—is that the cost to start advertising is much lower. (Just try to start advertising on the radio or TV for $50.) With online advertising, the results are immediate, and you can track precisely how your campaign is doing.

With traditional advertising you simply can't get all three of these benefits.

Does this mean online advertising that generates good results is easy? No.

It's very important to test your advertising to see what gets you the best results. As you repeatedly test, measure and refine your advertising, your results should get better and better, delivering more profitable results.

You want to test and measure the advertising copy itself—be it text or an image—and also test and measure the placement of your advertising. Should you advertise on web site A or web site B? Should you advertise on Facebook or a certain LinkedIn group?

Types of Advertising

There are two main types of advertising you'll encounter:

Cost Per Click advertising (CPC) wherein you only pay for the clicks generated by your advertising, or Cost per Million (CPM) advertising where you pay based on the number of impressions or eyes viewing your advertisement.

With CPC your advertisement might be seen by 10,000 people, but if only 5 click on it, that's what you pay. With CPM advertising, you pay for 10,000 people viewing your advertisement, whether they buy from you or not.

If you have a small budget and want to generate more immediate sales, CPC advertising is something you should consider—and this, in fact, is what is ideal for many smaller businesses. On the other hand, if you want to focus on brand building and making a huge impression, consider purchasing advertising based on CPM—you pay a fixed price for your advertisement to be displayed a certain number of times.

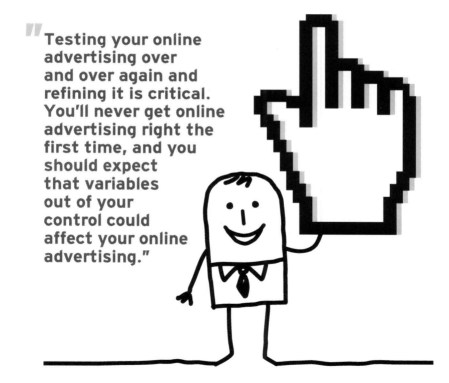

"Testing your online advertising over and over again and refining it is critical. You'll never get online advertising right the first time, and you should expect that variables out of your control could affect your online advertising."

Your advertising can be text (which is what many CPC advertisements are), images, or video. This is entirely up to the type of media allowed by the publisher your advertisement is served on.

Online Advertising Components
Advertising copy
The text or image you display in your advertisement is so important. If you do not have a compelling "call to action" (why should someone click on the advertisement or take the action you want them to), your advertising results will be low. Ensure you have the best message possible. Of course words like "free" and "sale" are time-tested words that draw attention.

Landing Pages
Landing pages are very important but often ignored parts of an online advertising campaign. When a customer clicks on your advertisement, where do they land? This is a landing page. If you've placed an advertisement for "yellow socks on sale" it make more sense (and cents) to have the shopper land on the page selling yellow socks that are on sale instead of landing on your clothing home page and having to find where the yellow socks on sale are.

Testing
Testing your online advertising over and over again and refining it is critical. You'll never get online advertising right the first time, and you should expect that variables out of your control (such as the news of the day, competition, regulatory issues, etc.) could affect your online advertising results. It's so important to test and measure the success of your online advertising so that you can constantly refine it. Maybe "free report" pulled in a better response than "50% off of report."

Targeting
Targeting your advertisement to the right audience is so important. Maybe you sell car covers. You might want to select several web sites and email newsletters that cater to toddlers. Create some advertising triggering their desire to keep their car "mess-free" from the cookie crumbs, Cheerios, and "spill-proof cups with the tops screwed on incorrectly." What about the traveling sales person who uses their car for sales and family? They might want to cover the seat during sales calls so the

seat stays fresh and new for the family's use after work. It's important that you not only find specific web sites that your audience might be viewing, but within those web sites, see if you can further narrow down your targeting by channel, theme, article genre, or video series.

Search Engine Optimization

You don't **have** to spend money in order to attract customers to your web site. You should take the time (or hire a consultant) to optimize your site for search engines. Whether you pay for advertising or not, ensure your web site is optimized for search engines.

Here are a few things to keep in mind:

Quality links

Quality links from other web sites are an important way for search engines to determine how relevant your web site is for a particular search result. It's just like when you are looking for a great vacation spot. You call your brother, your uncle, and your Aunt Mary in Nebraska. Your Aunt Mary recommends you call her girlfriend in New York City, and before you know it you've been able to narrow down your selection of vacation spots all because of trusted referrals from other people. Search engines rate your web site in a similar fashion. Imagine a web site like Politico.com. The more and more other web sites point to it, search engines "see" that it's a reliable source of quality information and give it a higher and higher ranking.

If you have good content on your web site (maybe a shopping guide for buying barbeque grills) and other web sites link to it, your ranking in the search engines will increase.

Don't try to get artificial links to your web site, like having your Mom's web site about casserole recipes link to your web site about seat covers. Search engines are pretty intelligent at sniffing out what's a real link and what's a "fake" link.

The more and better content you have, the more other web sites will link to you.

Content

Search engines love content. The more content—good content— you have on your web site, the higher your search engine ranking will go. Maybe you sell car engine parts. By having regular content that's all about car engines (and maybe other things as well), search engines will "detect" that your web site is a content-rich location for car engine information. The more information you have and the more frequent it is, the better your web site will look to search engines.

Pay Per Click Advertising
Google is the largest search engine, so it makes sense to spend some time and money in pay per click advertising on Google. Having said that, Bing, Yahoo, and other large portals have substantial and growing search traffic too. It's best to TEST and see which search portals work best for you and, in fact, you might want to proportionately spread out your PPC budget across several search engines.

Advertising Channels
Web Site
There are millions (zillions?) of web sites you can advertise on. It's important to know WHAT your audience is reading and what the most effective web sites to reach your audience are. You might not want to advertise on news sites or other "broad interest" web sites. Instead you might want to advertise on very vertically focused web sites, such as gaming, health, or entertainment.

Email Newsletters
Email newsletters are a powerful way to reach customers, directly to their inbox. Having your advertisement in an email newsletter sets a deep affinity of your message with the publisher. Email newsletters are a great way to have a lead generation campaign. For example: maybe you're a local real estate agent. You could advertise in the mortgage newsletter of the local credit union and offer a free home buying report.

Local Advertising
Local advertising is very important to millions of small businesses. In the first phase (as it were) of the web's development, the web was one big universe of web sites. The location of those businesses behind the web site was not that important.

However, search engines and related online products and services are ensuring that small businesses, who rely on local foot traffic to their places of business or telephone calls from local customers, are not only visible online but geographically indexed as well.

Type "flowers 66101" into your favorite search engine and guess what, you get a listing of florists near Kansas City, Kansas. Having an overall web presence is very important. However, if the main focus of your business is local, like a florist or plumber, it is important that you ensure your web site is listed as a local listing. Fewer and fewer people are licking their fingers and using the Yellow Pages. More people are using their phones and web browsers to find products and services from local businesses.

There are many services and solutions to help business advertise locally.

Yelp - http://www.yelp.com

Yelp's directory of local businesses, combined with local reviews, is something every business needs to take a look at. At the very least, ensure your Yelp profile, which could be there even if you have not put one there, is up to date and accurate. Oftentimes, Yelp's directory is found by Google before the web site of the actual business is. Looking for a pizza shop in Chicago? You'll probably find it indexed first on Yelp, before the pizza shop's own web site comes up. If you're in business, check out Yelp's business tools here: https://biz.yelp.com/

Google Places - http://www.google.com/places
Bizzy - http://www.bizzy.com
and Merchant Circle - http://www.merchantcircle.com

These services provide very small and local businesses with a web presence and a platform to engage local customers. You can have your own web site, but maybe you're a local hairdresser and a one-page web site or web page profile on one of these services is enough. These services—and keep in mind they all do vary in one way or the other but overall they guarantee your online presence—engage customers with photos, coupons, and they get insights on your local traffic.

8Coupons - http://www.8coupons.com

Services like 8Coupons let local customers get coupons (as in special deals) from your local business.

Group Buying Services

Group buying services such as Groupon (http://www.groupon.

com) and BuyWithMe (http://www.buywithme.com) let local businesses get a flood of new customers by offering very discounted deals. The deals are often a "buy one and get two free" type of offer (a VERY good and steeply discounted offer) but the deal ONLY kicks in when a certain number of customers sign up for the deal.

Retarget Advertising

Imagine what happens when a customer stops by your retail web site. They MIGHT browse around your web site for a few minutes and then most likely they leave.

This process is repeated over and over again on thousands of retail web sites all across the web.

Cost per click advertising (as well as marketing through email newsletters, blogs, and the like) can drive traffic to your web site. However, oftentimes, people browse first and then go to other web sites before buying. Or they go to other web sites completely unrelated to their purchase and forget about your web site altogether.

To help turn browsers into buyers and increase SALES (not just traffic), mediaFORGE, Retargeter (and other companies) have created an online advertising system that enables an advertisement to follow your "potential customer" around as they browse other web sites, reminding them of your web site.

In life, in general, most of the time, it takes more than one "poke" to get us to pay attention.

With retargeting technology, when customers leave your web site, you can still be in front of them, through a banner advertisement gently reminding them to come back and purchase.

What's also neat is that as customers fill up their shopping carts with items and buy from you (or decide not to buy) you can specifically target them with advertisements that complement what was in their shopping cart.

If you're looking to BOOST your online marketing, I would highly suggest you consider ad personalization and retargeting.

Social Media Advertising

Until recently, our focus has been on search engine marketing and banner advertising. Although these methods of advertising are still important, advertising on social media networks is also something to look at. Beyond building your own community on a social network, I'm referring to buying targeted advertising on LinkedIn, Facebook and, at some point, Twitter. See below for resources to help you do this.

The importance of using social media to communicate with your customers cannot be ignored. Hence in addition to LISTENING and COMMUNICATING through social media, you can also advertise.

Facebook and LinkedIn allow you to have very granular advertising options, taking advantage of the user profiles to display advertising to very specific audiences.

Twitter has a variety of advertising solutions. Its offers are relatively new and take place in the form of promoted Tweets, Trends, and Accounts. If you are looking to build your Twitter followers and want to engage more deeply with users and make them aware of your tweets, trending topics, or Twitter account, you may want to consider advertising with Twitter. It's important to let an expert help you navigate through your options.

You'll only know which of the many avenues of advertising work for you if you test and measure your campaigns to determine which solution works best for you.

Mobile Advertising
More of your prospective customers are using their smartphones or regular cell phones and not their computers. This is a new opportunity and challenge for your business. Always consider where your customers are and follow them. I'm not saying to forsake traditional online advertising, but I am advising you to explore other advertising solutions.

Mobile advertising includes several options:
» Advertising (banner or text) on the mobile web sites of web publishers.
» Advertising within mobile games or other applications
» Send special deals or other messages to current or prospective customers via TXT or SMS. Be very careful when you do this so you don't spam customers or antagonize them. We get enough advertising (or spam) through emails; the sending of sponsored communication via TXT or SMS should be done carefully.
» Mobile search is one of the most commonly performed actions on mobile devices. People are searching for information, entertainment, things to buy, and more. Your advertisement should be there at the moment someone is doing a query on the keyword of relevance to your business.

There are several actions you can encourage a user to take, based on your mobile advertisement:

> » Click to call
> » Click to order
> » Click to buy
> » Click to download
> » And more...

The most powerful form of advertising is often your existing customers giving you a good recommendation or referral to prospective customers."

You could also have users TXT (instead of call) to initiate the action. As in: Text 5555 to receive the free guide or to participate in a survey.

The mobile marketing association gives the following differences between mobile advertising and computer advertising:

The mobile phone is a highly targeted device with typically one user. As such, powerfully accurate and relevant communication messages can be delivered where users become instantly engaged with campaigns and content resulting in increased campaign effectiveness.

The environment in which people interact with their mobile phone does not lend itself to detailed information search and delivery. Instead, mobile users seek quick and convenient access to information and services when they are out and about. Space on the mobile phone screen is at a premium, and users have limited input mechanisms, so mobile web sites need to be easy to navigate using just the mobile phone keypad.

Today's mobile phones have a broad range of different form factors, screen sizes, and resolutions, all of which present a challenge for the display and optimal viewing of content and advertising. This book's recommendations directly address this challenge.

Referral Marketing

As you are seeking to acquire new customers, don't forget that the most powerful form of advertising is often your existing customers giving you a good recommendation or referral to prospective customers. Use referral services such as FavRav (Facebook Application), Grasshopper Group's Spreadable, Ratepoint, and other tools to help boost and enable referrals from customers.

Online Marketing and Advertising Resources

There is so much to learn and know when it comes to online advertising. Some resources you should consider are:

Wilson Web
http://www.wilsonweb.com

Clickz.com
http://www.clickz.com

Google Online Courses in Online Advertising
http://services.google.com/ads_inquiry/awseminars

Advertise on Facebook
http://www.facebook.com/advertising/

Advertise on LinkedIn
http://www.linkedin.com/static?key=advertising_info

Advertise on Twitter
http://support.twitter.com/groups/35-business

Mobile Advertising
http://www.mobilemarketingwatch.com/resource-guides/

Mobile Marketing Association
http://mmaglobal.com/
(check out their resource guides)

Google and the Small Business Administration
have partnered to educate local businesses about how to succeed online. Each video describes how a small business owner successfully uses the internet to grow his business. It's important to be where your customers are: online. Check out http://www.google.com/help/places/partners/sba/ to see an overview of a variety of tools for web analytics, paid online advertising, free online marketing, web sites, images, and more.

CHAPTER 8:
Email Marketing

Email marketing is one of the most powerful forms of marketing. It enables you to build relationships with current customers and attract new customers through email.

Email marketing is relatively easy thanks to the many companies that offer email marketing services.

Dating Your Leads and Marrying Your Customers

For current customers, a good email newsletter keeps your brand (products, services, name) in front of them on a regular basis. When they go to buy from your competition, or when they forget to buy, your newsletter gives you the opportunity to capture a sale.

A newsletter to current customers can also be informational and be used to a) build loyalty so customers keep you in mind as the expert or "the business of record" for their needs b) can help build demand for your products and services.

For example: if you have a pet grooming business, a good newsletter can help keep your customers coming back to you, again and again, when they have the need for your services. Maybe customers don't know how often they need to have their pets professionally groomed; a good newsletter can help educate them on this need—providing you more sales.

For potential customers, an email newsletter is a powerful tool for those who might not be ready to buy "immediately"—your newsletter keeps you in their mind and when they are ready to buy, they are "pre-sold." Maybe you are not ready to take a vacation today, but by getting the ski newsletter from Vermont, when you are ready for a vacation, you'll definitely check out a ski trip in Vermont.

Email Newsletter Marketing Tips
Your Audience
As you consider your email marketing strategy, think about your audience. Who are you writing to? Are you writing to current customers? Are you writing to prospective customers? Are you writing to employees? Are you writing to single mothers about their children's education or are you writing to grandparents about gift ideas for their grand children?

The audience you are writing to should directly impact the message you write.

Frequency
Do not send your newsletter too frequently, or people will un-subscribe. Don't send it too infrequently either, as you won't be at the forefront of your customer's mind when it comes time for them to buy. Think of your newsletter as going to a distant relative's home. Visiting them every once in a while and engaging them in a good conversation or bringing them a treat is most welcome. But coming every day, and being a total bore or drinking all their milk is distasteful and a waste of their time (and yours).

Design
Make sure the overall design looks good. If you have to have a professional designer make your newsletter look great, it's worth the investment. Each issue makes an impression on your business and should be well-designed. No clutter. Lots of white space. No spelling errors. Good English. Etc., etc.

▶▶ The audience you are writing to should directly impact the message you write."

Content

The content of your e-newsletter is critical and should be carefully considered. Think about the newsletters that you receive. Which ones do you really enjoy receiving? Many newsletters are information-based. Some newsletters are more "hard sale" formatted and contain updates on what products are on sale. There is no right or wrong way; it all depends on what is best for your audience and generates the best response for your business.

For information-based newsletters, consider the following suggestions:

- » Highlight your customers. Write about their businesses and include information on how they are using your product or service in their business.
- » Write information related to your product. If you sell soccer balls, why not include information not only on the best soccer balls to buy, but also on soccer clinics and camps, upcoming high school games, and how to get tickets to professional games?
- » Show your readers how to get the most out of your product or service. Maybe you are a graphics design firm and have an email newsletter. Consider offering tips to your readers about what makes great design and what makes terrible design. Show them examples.

Subject Line

Your subject line is one of the MOST important parts of your email message. Your subject line is the FIRST thing your audience will see and what will cause them to initially open your email. If your subject line does not engage the reader, does not catch their eye, does not cause them to WANT to open the email, your email open rates (therefore the action rate overall) will be quite low. Pay very, very careful attention to the subject line. Think carefully on what the subject line will be.

Permission

Don't build your email list subscription base with email address of people who have not opted in to receive your email newsletter. First of all it is illegal[4] and secondly it's not ethical.

---

4   http://smallbiztechnology.com/archive/2009/01/
power-email-marketing-the-thre.html

Why Use An Email Marketing Service?

For those of you who are emailing your customers through the "bcc" or "cc" field of your email program (like Outlook), this is okay when you are emailing 1 or 2 people. But it's best to use the services of an email marketing company for a number of reasons:

» They work hard to ensure your email gets through the spam and "black list" filters
» They help you manage who signs up to and un-subscribes to your newsletter
» They give you statistics on who opened your newsletter and/or click on various links in the newsletter

Beyond Email Marketing As Usual[5]

Maybe you are already doing email marketing pretty well. My guess is there is room for improvement. To take your marketing to another level, implement targeting and personalization and focusing on improving the delivery—ensuring the email reaches each subscriber and is not blocked by spam.

Targeting

Instead of having one email newsletter for every person who signs up, consider segmenting your readers into two, three (or more) profiles so that each email newsletter is more customized for them.

Email list segmentation has moved from being a marketing buzzword to a best practice among many small businesses. Increased segmentation can improve the relevance and targeting of small business email marketing campaigns. Small businesses should make a conscious effort to use basic and advanced list-building features and technologies offered by the top email marketing services, which allow them to create multiple, highly customized lists based on specific audience attributes.

Personalization

While targeting is useful, personalization takes things up to another level. Maybe you have a store catering to fishing. Why not send all your customers an email address to them by name

---

5 http://smallbiztechnology.com/archive/2009/01/
power-email-marketing-the-thre.html

(well that's easy—most of us do that anyway) but also reminding them of their past purchase and suggestions for future purchases—all automatically personalized to each client. This brings email to life and makes it much more than just a transaction.

Like segmentation, small businesses have long understood the value of personalizing their email marketing communications, but have lagged behind larger organizations with more sophisticated and advanced marketing technologies. In 2008, more small businesses took the simple, but important step of not only using mail merge functions to ensure that each email salutation is addressed to the individual, but also using list attribute features that allow them to personalize messages according to stored personal attributes such as demographics and buying behavior.

Deliverability

You set up a great email marketing campaign and do all you can to segment your lists, but what if no one receives (or many people don't receive) it because it was blocked by spam filters or some other problem? It is so important to ensure the message you take careful plans to create REACHES the recipients.

" 70 percent of survey respondents cited email deliverability services as more important than cost (69 percent) when selecting an email marketing service."

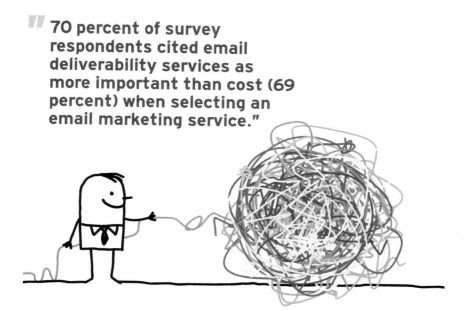

Despite a plethora of industry studies confirming email marketing's effectiveness and unbeatable ROI, deliverability concerns persist among businesses of all sizes. According to Jupiter Research's Email Marketing Buyer's Guide, 2008, 70 percent of survey respondents cited email deliverability services as more important than cost (69 percent) when selecting an email marketing service.

If you are not doing email marketing, START. If you already have an email newsletter—it can always be improved.

Email Marketing Resources

Taste of Technology for Small Businesses Email Marketing (event video)
http://smallbiztechnology.com/tasteoftechnology/emailmarketing08/

Email Marketing Webinar Series
http://www.smallbiztechnology.com/webinar

Campaigner's Resources for Email Marketing
http://www.campaigner.com/education.aspx

Constant Contact Email Marketing Learning Center
http://www.constantcontact.com/learning-center/index.jsp

Mail Chimp Email Marketing Resources
http://www.mailchimp.com/resources

Vertical Response Email Marketing Guides and Articles
http://www.verticalresponse.com/education-support/guides/

CHAPTER 9

Blogging for Businesss

Blogs are one of the oldest forms of online communications after web sites and emails. They're easy to start but not easy to be successful at.

To start, simply sign on with one of the dozens of blogging services such as Wordpress, Movabletype, TypePad, or Blogger.com. Select a template (how your blog should look) and you're ready.

The hard part is deciding what content you want to publish on your blog. Is it going to be a daily blog with a very short post of your thoughts? Will it be a monthly post highlighting how your favorite customers are using your product? Will it contain videos or photos? You have a lot of options, but like an email newsletter, just make sure you know who your audience is and what they want.

Blogs offer a variety of benefits:
- » Boost your rankings in the search engines
- » Give fresh content to your web site
- » Help you engage with your customers
- » If you blog well and regularly, the content will position you as an expert

When you create your blog, you can host your blog on the (often free) platform of the blog provider (such as Wordpress or TypePad). However, there are two other options: Get a domain name for your blog (such as http://www.rayreport.com, which is a Wordpress blog). If you want to add more content and freshness to your static web site, you could integrate your blog into your web site using embed code or RSS feeds. (Speak to a local social media guru for help on this if you need to.)

Fresh Content

There are very few people who love to eat stale food. In the same way, there are few people who enjoy visiting a stale web site that looked the same in 2001, 2002, 2003, 2004, 2005 and 2009! Having a blog, which makes it easy for you and any other authorized person to update your web site, can help add fresh content to your otherwise dull web site. Think about it: how often are you going to change the "about us" page?

Having fresh content attracts not only an audience of customers and prospective customers, especially if the content is useful and interesting, but it also attracts the search engines.

Search engines that see a web site is freshly updated and linked to by other web sites place the web site in a higher ranking.

Community and Communication

Another benefit of a blog is that it enables you to communicate with your audience more quickly and have features such as commenting. Commenting is an important way to get input from your customers. Imagine blogging about how a customer used your special hair oil and received comments on how rich and luscious their hair looks. What if other customers write in on their experiences and maybe even another customer or two writes in about their not-so-good experience?

What have you gained?

- » You create a dialogue with your customers and gain valuable feedback from them
- » You enable customers to communicate with you and communicate with each other
- » New customers gain confidence in buying your product from reading what others write about your product
- » New customers can shop as informed customers. Maybe the hair oil is NOT good for them. Instead of having a customer buy the product and return it for a refund, it's better that they don't buy the product (but of course buy something else!).

BLOG TIP: It's important to integrate your blog with your web site. Every time you blog a new post, you want to have at least the headline somewhere on the main part of your web site. This will ensure that search engines not only index your blog but also your main web site.

Blogging Resources

Duct Tape Marketing Video on Blogging For Business 101
http://www.ducttapemarketing.com/blog/2009/10/09/small-business-blogging-101/

Type Pad Tips for Better Blogging
http://www.typepad.com/tips/

CHAPTER 10:
Video For Business

While email, web sites, and other types of "text" communication are very good, nothing beats the power of video.

Why is it that millions of us sit glued to a TV or computer screen every evening? Why is it that instead of playing football, millions of men (and women) sit like rabid wolves in front of a caged deer watching the Super Bowl every year? Why do we spend billions of dollars at movie theatres, with Netflix (my wife's favorite), and Amazon.com (my favorite), and Blockbuster buying movies?

We all love video.

Using video in your business is no different. Sending your client a video presentation, or a video clip of how you can really lay down their asphalt or how a new suit looks on them, is much better than trying to "show" them via an email message.

Video is also a good marketing tactic. Maybe you have a funny video or a very powerful presentation. Your client or employees won't keep it to themselves; they'll send it to friends, post it on Facebook, etc.

Video used to be something that only very large companies could do. They had the expertise, the expensive digital equipment, the facilities to host the video, and the means to market the video to make it worthwhile to create in the first place.

Over the past few years, especially with the rise of Youtube (and other online video sharing/storing services) and lower costs of video equipment, EVERY small business can now create their own videos.

Expertise

Expertise is NOT needed to create video. There are dozens of free and low-cost programs that you can learn to use in one sitting (or ask a sharp employee to do so). Windows XP comes with a free video editing tool. You won't compete against Steven Spielberg, but you will create video for your business.

Video Equipment

Video equipment? Expensive? You can get a Flip Video[6] camera, made by Pure Digital Technologies, for $129 from Amazon.com. I bought one and love it. Of course you can get a more expensive camera (including accessories), video editing software, and lighting equipment. But before investing too much, learn more about the process of creating great video.

> ❚❚ **Once you create the video, getting people to watch the video should not be a problem. Make sure it's visible on your web site, linked to on your blog, uploaded to your social media page, and more."**

6   www.theflip.com

Hosting

Hosting video is definitely not an expensive option. You can create your own channel on Youtube, Flickr, Vimeo, Blip.tv, or dozens of other services. These services are free. Services like Brightcove and Viddler, which are fee-based, provide more professional options to manage, host, and monetize your videos.

Once you create the video, getting people to watch the video should not be a problem. Make sure it's visible on your web site, linked to on your blog, uploaded to your social media page, and more. Blendtec's Willitblend.com is a good example of how a video series became popular. To showcase how powerful their blender is, they started blending all sorts of non-food items—including an iPhone. The videos became popular and were shared all over the Internet (viral marketing).

Two Neat Video Services

1. **Pixability** – If you want help creating a professionally edited video, Pixability will send you a Flip camera to record your video. Send them back the Flip camera and they'll professionally edit your video.
2. **Turn Here** – If you want help getting a video production team together to create a professional video for your business, Turn Here brings together an entire production team to help.

Video Resources

10 Tips To Create Your "Remarkable" Corporate Video
http://www.directortom.com/director-tom/2007/3/10/10-tips-to-create-your-remarkable-corporate-video.html

---

CHAPTER 11:
Software as a Service (SaaS)

Software As A Service (also known as Cloud Computing or Hosted Applications) is the technology that enables you to access services through a web browser rather than a traditionally installed local computer program. Instead of installing software on your computer, you open your web browser and access the application you need by going to a web address.

With hosted applications, there are many benefits:

- » No software to install
- » Faster rollout of software to remote users or other users who are local
- » No conflicts with existing software
- » No worry about having the most recent version of software. The software is always the most recent
- » Easier to connect various software services to each other through back-end interfaces. Meaning: your CRM service can connect to your email service seamlessly, with less effort than a traditional software package would take
- » Less upfront cost. Instead of paying huge license fees or paying for expensive installation or consulting services, hosted applications are often low-cost monthly fees, sometimes even free
- » More availability of a variety of services from more providers. There are very few cash management or accounting solutions for small businesses. However, there are dozens of competing online services.

How Cloud Computing Helped Boost Productivity In the Mountains of Pennsylvania

Last week I was at a weekend retreat for young men and I was managing registration.

I packed a small suitcase of clothing and three other bags of gear: Scanner from Wasp Bar Code, Verizon Wireless MiFi (portable WiFi hotspot), and an array of other gadgets and gizmos, including my Dell Latitude (on loan from Dell).

The highlight of the technology we used for the weekend was online collaboration (Google Docs) which allowed us to NOT have to setup a network, yet instantly and seamlessly share files.

> ❞ **The world of hosted applications (or cloud computing), like never before, enables you and those you need to collaborate with to connect."**

The power of hosted applications for growing companies who want to grow fast, save money, and be more productive (sound like you?) requires using tools that will enable this to happen.

At the retreat, five other organizers and I were able to access a shared spreadsheet and see updated changes in real time. If we had used the traditional model of using a word processor we would have had to email the file back and forth and risk not having the most updated information on any one computer.

The world of hosted applications (or cloud computing), like never before, enables you and those you need to collaborate with to connect.

I think about the evolving video sharing platform of Brightcove or other video hosting services. You can do some pretty neat things with your video, and no software to install in your computer.

What about Picasa? This powerful online photo sharing platform lets you share one or hundreds of photos with others. What's even better, it has a software tool you can download to manage your video collection offline.

I've been using Dropbox which enables me to share files with anyone else, or easily access files when I'm away from my desktop. This is the beauty of hosted applications.

These are just a few of the MANY applications the businesses can use, through the power of a web browser, to enhance their daily productivity and communication with customers, employees, and partners.

The key to using hosted applications is to find the application(s) that best work for YOU. There are hundreds of applications for your business—you only need to be concerned with the ones that solve your business pain points.

9 Questions To Ask Before Moving To Cloud Computing

Although so many businesses are using cloud computing services (email hosting, security, inventory, employee management, and more), there are still many businesses who are cautious about moving the entire business to a hosted environment.

They have reasons to be concerned. *Business Week* put together 9 questions that you could (and should) ask your hosting provider before forking your data over to them:

1. Who else might see the data?
2. What if you don't pay the bill?
3. Does the cloud back up your data?
4. What if your service provider enters your business?
5. What if you do business abroad?
6. What does the cloud expect of you?
7. What's the access control?
8. Do you want your employees getting advertising (perhaps from competitors, or for naughty products) along with their e-mail?
9. What is your exit strategy?

Read the full Business Week article here: http://www.business-week.com/technology/content/aug2008/tc2008083_703047.htm?link_position=link14

What Services Are Ideal For Cloud Computing

Cloud computing is ideal for every software that you now use. The ONLY exception would be applications that require intensive computing power and work with large files. For example, video games, graphic and video editing, and other related software are not ideal for most cloud computing services. However, as broadband gets faster and as developers develop better and faster cloud computing, ALL computing—with no exception—can be done online.

Office Productivity Applications

Microsoft Office, and prior to that Corel World Perfect, is one of the leading business productivity applications in the market. However, Microsoft, Google Apps/Docs, Zoho, Hyper Office, Cisco Web Office, and dozens of other companies now offer competing suites for word processing, spreadsheets, presentations, and more.

Many other vendors make single applications that are designed for databases (Intuit QuickBase, Dabble DB, Trackvia, Caspio), presentations (Slide Rocket), and other uses and are only in the cloud.

Accounting / Cash Management

Similar to office productivity applications, small business accounting and cash flow management software has been led by Intuit QuickBooks and Sage Peachtree. However, thanks to the rise of online applications, these vendors (Intuit and Sage) now have online accounting tools but they are also joined by Fresh Books, Indinero, Outright, NetSuite, and many others who have varying degrees of online accounting solutions.

Collaboration and Communication

Collaboration and communication are a big part of what businesses need to do. We need to work with our team of employees, outside vendors, consultants, and of course, customers. We share files, share calendars, manage projects, need-to-do lists, and so much more. There are hundreds of tools and services, with varying degrees of functionality, to help you do these things and more. The tools that provide office productivity (listed above) all have elements of collaboration and communication functionalities. For file sharing (and for some, a bit more), check out Dropbox, Dropio, OfficeDrop, Yousendit.com, and others.

What Other SaaS Tools Should You Consider?
  » CRM/Contact Management: BatchBlue, Infusion Soft, Zoho CRM, ACT!
  » Email Marketing: Campaigner, Vertical Response, Mail Chimp, Constant Contact

There are many more hosted application services for your business, such as mobile applications, inventory, sales and lead management, billing, field service management, project and task management, retail services, ecommerce, billing, and so much more.

The categories in the preceding paragraph are categories listed in the Small Business Web. Don't know what it is?

What is the "Small Business Web"?

I would be remiss if I did not mention The Small Business Web: http://www.thesmallbusinessweb.com

The Small Business Web is an online directory created by a confederation of five founding companies whose mission is to ensure that the member companies enable data to be easily shared with each other. This means that the data in your CRM vendor can easily and seamlessly share data with the data in your email marketing vendor.

Their press release reads:

"The Small Business Web aims to: Bring together like-minded, customer-obsessed software companies to integrate our respective products and make life easier for small businesses. While there are many products available for small business owners on the Web, the approach we're taking is to use each others APIs to provide a high-level of integration between these applications and create a more seamless experience for our customers."

Chatting with Sunir Shah, Chief Handshaker from FreshBooks, it seems that the initiative is all about providing a complete set of integrations—all players integrating with each other—rather than simple two-way integrations. They believe in doing so they've begun to create a complete offering, a "web of SaaS" for SMBs. Think of a best-of-breed suite that is customized to a particular user's needs.

The initiative members seem pretty bullish about the value to be gained from The Small Business Web—it somehow preempts the sort of easy integrations that SaaS have been promising since their inception. It also goes someway to addressing the concerns that led to Martin Kleppmann's OAccounts initiative—that is a simple, easy, and consistent way of integrating different small business applications.

Of course there's always a flip side to this approach—the duplication within the businesses (separate marketing and overhead, etc.) is going to have an impact on the cost of the suite—until now it's been easy to justify a few $20 subscriptions per month here and there. However, when we look at a suite made up of a number of different applications, that price ticket can grow pretty rapidly. The jury is out on how well businesses will cope with a $100 or $200 "suite" of SaaS products—especially when some of the other players are providing close to the functionality of all of the separate offerings, but at a lower total cost.

In response to these concerns, I was told that the idea of the web is not that customers will buy all the products. It's that there is a real ecosystem forming and customers will pick the software that plays well with all their other tools over those that are disconnected. That's a powerful selling point and it will be interesting to see which other players join the initiative.

Either way, integration is good, as is enabling efficiencies for small businesses—the Small Business Web is definitely one to watch.

Software As A Service Resources

How Cloud Computing Can Help Small Businesses (Business Week)
http://www.businessweek.com/magazine/content/09_68/s0908060315092.htm

What Cloud Computing Means for Small Businesses (Read Write Web)
http://www.readwriteweb.com/archives/what_cloud_computing_means_for_small_businesses.php

Should You Move Your Business To the Cloud (PC World)
http://www.pcworld.com/businesscenter/article/188173/should_you_move_your_small_business_to_the_cloud.html;jsessionid=37C121AF50A4C2E6A54DF2E0AB22F829

Small Business Guide to Cloud Computing (Small Business Trends)
http://smallbiztrends.com/2010/11/16-questions-to-ask-yourself-before-choosing-cloud-computing-solutions.html

CHAPTER 12:
Printers

Buying a printer is an important investment and there are many factors to consider as you choose which printer or printers might work best for your office.

Although we aim to have a "paperless office", it's inevitable that we need to print a document and hold something in our hand. As you consider your next printer, the major decision you'll have to decide is whether you should buy a laser printer or ink jet printer. You might want to have low-cost black and white laser printers on the desk of each employee and have a fast and much larger color printer for each work group.

Speed

When buying a printer, consider the speed at which it prints. How fast each sheet of paper prints is just as important as how long it takes for the printer to warm up (in the case of a laser printer) and print the first page after you have given the "print" command from your computer.

Paper Handling

The options for paper handling are also important. Do you want to do duplex printing? If you do a lot of printing, you may want to consider having a large paper tray so you don't have to add paper so often. Also consider what type of paper you'll be printing on. If you need A4 paper, legal paper, or specialty sized paper, ensure your printer can handle it.

Ink and Toner

When deciding between ink jet and laser jet, the cost of ink/toner is also something to think about. If you print hundreds to thousands of pages per month, you'll probably be better off printing from a laser printer, as their toner cartridges print more paper per cartridge, compared to a the much smaller ink jet cartridge.

Color or Black and White

Pound for pound and feature for feature, a black and white printer is going to be less expensive than a color printer. However, when deciding on whether to purchase black and white or color, don't let price be your only consideration. Is it going to be a laser printer or ink jet printer? Is it going to print very fast?

Every office should have at least one (one per every few employees) black and white workgroup printer. This printer will be your day-to-day printer, used for drafts and for client proposals. Since there's only one toner or ink cartridge to change, the day-to-day use of the machine will be easier to maintain as well.

A color printer is ideal for those times when black and white simply won't do. Remember when you received that spreadsheet full of numbers and someone nicely highlighted certain rows or numbers for you? You need that printed in a color printer. Or what about the corporate sales brochure or newsletter with the colored font and crisp photos? Only a color printer will do.

Ink Jet or Laser Jet

Ink Jet printers spray ink through nozzles on a print head to get ink onto the paper, and the end result is usually not as sharp as a laser printout. Laser printers used to be very expensive so ink jets were a cheaper option. But with laser jet prices being so low and printing much crisper and faster, it makes sense to purchase a laser printer for your office (and home).

Multi-function Printers

Multi-function printers (MPS) are great options for small workgroups or home offices that want to have a scanner, fax machine, and printer all in one place.

These devices are compact, so they save space and reduce the tangle of wires spread among three different devices.

While much of the focus on printing is on traditional hardware printers, keep in mind that outsourced printing solutions from 48HourPrint, MagCloud, and VistaPrint can also be considered. Maybe you need 400 copies of a company flyer printed, printing on your desktop printer is one option, but you may also want to see the cost (and time) effectiveness of printing it through one of these outsourced printing services.

Printer Buying Resources

PrintCountry.com's Printer Buying Guide
http://www.printcountry.com/resources/
Printer_Buying_Guide.pdf

CHAPTER 13

Money Saving Tips for Your Business When Investing in Technology

When investing money in IT solutions for your business, the end result could be that you end up boosting productivity, saving money, increasing customer satisfaction, and other benefits of the proper implementation of technology in your business.

On the other hand, you might invest $50,000 in new computer equipment and find your return on investment is a gain of 0 or that you in fact LOSE money on the investment. Maybe it's a new computer system and the software does not work correctly and customers' orders are getting mixed up. In this case, you'll end up losing business and possibly lose employees too.

Here are a few tips from CDW to help you save money using the technology in your business:

Purchase and Support:
» Negotiate prices and look for bulk purchase rates on systems, software, and support contracts.
» Consider replacing all PCs in the same year; you'll see deeper discounts.
» Sticking primarily with one IT vendor can often result in better overall deals.
» Find the lowest available posted prices, then ask for even lower prices.

Power, Cooling, and Space:
» Upgrading Uninterruptible Power Supplies (UPSs) to newer energy-efficient units can cut energy use and save money.
» To save power, have the staff turn off their monitors, task lights, etc. on nights and weekends, while leaving the CPU running.
» Use blanking panels in server racks and "air locking" grommets in raised-floor panels to minimize cold air loss.
» House servers in a "cooling closet" or other area where they can be "spot-cooled" instead of using general office air conditioning.

IT system/network administration/management:
» Have your IT vendor pre-configure and asset tag products prior to delivery to your office.
» Have your IT vendor configure or "ghost" your software onto hardware products prior to delivery.
» Make use of hardware and software asset management tracking, often available free from your IT vendor.
» Use free tools like Microsoft's Software Update Services (SUS) patch management to keep systems up to date.
» Create system images of your configurations, i.e. using Symantec Ghost, to restore systems instead of rebuilding/reinstalling software.
» Use LogMeIn software to access or control a PC or Mac from a distance.

» Consider outsourcing IT network administration for installation, support, maintenance, and repair.

Hardware:
Servers
» Consolidate servers by using blades and virtualization to replace old, inefficient units, thereby saving money on power, cooling, and space.
» Bring in applications that can run on your current server along with other applications to avoid having to buy another server, and save on power and cooling.

Desktops, Notebooks
» Buy desktop computers for office-based employees; they can deliver more power and value for your IT dollar.
» Save money purchasing three desktop computers for what it might cost you to buy two notebook computers.
» When purchasing PCs, sacrificing some CPU speed while adding extra RAM can increase the value of your IT purchase.
» Buy notebook PCs for mobile and non-desk-oriented employees to garner the added productivity of working from anywhere.
» When applicable, consider smartphones and Portable Digital Assistants (PDAs) for staff who may not need a notebook PC.

Monitors
» Replace CRT monitors with LCD monitors that use a lot less power (as much as 60 percent) and generate less heat, thereby cutting electricity and cooling costs.
» Buy the largest LCD monitor that makes sense as more screen space often translates into increased productivity.
» Multitask using dual monitors on the desktop to save time closing and reopening applications or switching between windows.
» Set power-management and screensavers so that computers and monitors power down when not used for a designated period of time.

Software:

» Take advantage of money-saving software volume licensing programs often available for as few as five desktop PCs.

» Implement time-saving software license tracking and management, often available at no charge from your software vendor.

» When possible, switch from software licensing covering "total users" to "number of active users" in order to save on fees.

» Consider open-source software as your server, and even desktop operating system, as a way to possibly cut costs.

Networking and Communications:

» Consider web-managed switches (smart switches) offering many features of managed switches at close to unmanaged switch prices.

» Avoid the cost of dropping cables by equipping your office with a wireless (802.11 Wi-Fi) network.

» Add to office productivity by saving staff the time and hassle of having to delete unwanted e-mail by using anti-spam filtering software.

Telephony:

» Switch your phone service to Voice over Internet Protocol (VoIP), and save nearly 40% on local calls and as much as 90% on international calling.

» Save about 40 percent in cabling costs for new buildings by using VoIP for telephone service.

» Use the same staffer for network, data, and telephone setup and maintenance by switching to VoIP telephone services.

» When appropriate, use Skype for collaboration (conference calling), especially for international calls.

» Use audio, video, and multimedia conferencing and collaboration software and web services as an alternative to expensive travel.

Storage:

- » Instead of file servers, use lower-powered, lower-cost, and easier-to-administer Networked Attached Storage (NAS) appliances.
- » If you have a lot of files, consider de-duplication software to reduce space demands and eliminate the need to purchase extra storage.

Printers:

- » Use multifunction printers (MFPs) combining copy, print, scan, and fax functions to eliminate having to purchase individual devices.
- » Consider a color printer for small print runs to save the time and cost of using an outside print shop.
- » Multifunction printer (MFPs) can help save money on print consumables (paper, toner, etc.).
- » Multifunction printers (MFPs) take up a small footprint, thereby saving office space and possibly cost.
- » Networked multifunction printers (MFPs), strategically located in a workgroup, can help save money by eliminating the need to purchase extra printers.
- » Use printer management software to limit the use of more costly color printing to designated individuals, time of day, etc.
- » Save on paper by promoting two-up (two page images per side) and duplex (both sides of the paper) printing, as well as the reuse of sheets.
- » Save on paper by having the staff print only the pages of documents and web sites that they need.
- » Consider non-brand printer consumables; recycle used cartridges; and look for rebates and other price reductions.
- » Small energy-efficient print servers can reduce power use and take up less space compared to older, larger print servers.

Summary

In the past several thousand words and dozens of paragraphs, I've tried my best to educate you, to whet your appetite about some of the key technologies and strategies and how to implement them so that you can use technology as a tool to grow your business.

Technology can be VERY confusing and challenging. It can be a darn pain. However, if you embrace it, like good exercise and healthy eating, you'll find that it will propel your business forward, make you more competitive, and endear customers to you and your brand.

Technology—the right use, the strategic use of technology—is the key that will make your business move smarter, move faster, be more productive, increase revenue, save time, boost profit, and enhance customer service.

Don't be afraid. Embrace technology.

Don't do it all yourself. Hire an expert (or more than one) to help you with various segments of your technology implementation.

Acknowledgments

Special thanks to:

Laura Leites
www.Smallbiztechnology.com
for reviewing and editing

Vicky Montenegro
www.curiouscreatives.com
for the great design work

Editorial contributions from:

Jane Tabachnik
Marketing Consultant
http://www.janetabachnick.com

Mardy Sitzer
Marketing Consultant
Bumblebee Design & Marketing LLC
www.bumblebeellc.com

Brent Leary
Journalist, Writer, IT Analyst, CRM and
Social Media Guru
CRM Essentials
www.crm-essentials.com

Gene Marks
IT Consultant
Gene Marks LLC
http://www.marksgroup.net/

Smallbiztechnology.com Events

It is Smallbiztechnology.com's mission to educate growing companies about how to use technology as tool to further the growth of their business. We do this through events and online content.

Following is a list of some of our upcoming live and online events. You can get more info on these events and more by subscribing to the weekly email Small Business Technology Report.
http://smallbiztechnology.com/emailnewsletter

Small Biz Tech Tour 2011

Our second annual series of nationwide events will be stopping in five cities - Mountain View, CA, Salt Lake City, Washington, DC, Atlanta and Boston in the fall of 2011.

At each full day event you'll network with your peers. Learn from experts. Speak with technology vendors. Participate in discussions. Eat. Win Prizes. And more - all with the goal of seeing how you can leverage technology and empower your business for growth.
http://www.smallbiztechtour.com

Seventh Annual Small Business Summit 2012

Scheduled for March 13, 2012 in New York City, the Summit is attended by over 450 growing companies, media, SMB and tech experts, and small business influencers. See the HOT Tech Demo and find out the winner of this year's Small Business Strategy Award. Eat, network with other entrepreneurs, win prizes and learn.
http://smallbiztechsummit.com

Webinars

Our monthly evening webinar series features awesome business and technology experts sharing their knowledge through info-packed presentations and informal discussions with us and the live audience.

View some of our past webinar recordings http://smallbiztechnology.com/webinar

Taste of Technology Series

These monthly live events held in New York City are the ultimate blend of information and networking. Business owners gather at these evening events to educate themselves on a variety of technologies that will help them grow their businesses. Panels of expert speakers discuss a specific topic for each event.
http://smallbiztechnology.com/tasteoftechnology

12 Hours of Tech at New York Internet Week

This full day event on June 8, 2011 during Internet Week features 12 Hours of educational content presented by experts covering a wide range of different technologies that growing companies need to know about, from video to text marketing to local online marketing and more. http://12hoursoftech.com

Small Biz Tech Pavilion at New York XPO
New York City, November 16, 2011. We host a technology pavilion featuring a small theater on the New York XPO show floor. The full day agenda features short information sessions and interviews with small business experts and tech gurus, all of which are videotaped and shown on Smallbiztechnology.com. Learn, contribute, and mingle with NY XPO's 15,000+ attendees.

Small Biz | Big Things
This two day, premier, national event in San Francisco is focused on helping growing businesses keep the customers they have, obtain new customers and leverage technology as a tool to grow their businesses. Produced by Smallbiztechnology.com and as an outgrowth of the successful Small Business Summit in New York City, Small Biz | Big Things brings together leading small business experts, small business vendors and service providers, and of course small business owners themselves for 2 days of insight, networking, exhibits and fun. Stay tuned to Smallbiztechnology.com for more information

REMEMBER TO SIGN UP FOR YOUR WEEKLY, FREE Small Business Technology Report email newsletter http://smallbiztechnology.com/emailnewsletter

About Smallbiztechnology.com
Smallbiztechnology.com is a media company educating small, growing business, in how to strategically use technology as a tool to further grow their businesses. This education is done through content and events.

Smallbiztechnology.com is all about helping "regular" small business owners - those who are not technically savvy - know what technology they need to boost productivity, save time, save time, increase revenue and boost customer service in their business.

CHECK OUT
Ramon Ray's videos at http://www.youtube.com/smallbiz_technology

CPSIA information can be obtained
at www.ICGtesting.com
Printed in the USA
LVIW011901250412
279111LV00001B